LEARN TO NAVIGATE GOD'S PRESENCE AND EXPERIENCE HEAVEN ON EARTH

JOSEPH DARATONY

MINDSTIR MEDIA

*LEARN TO NAVIGATE GOD'S PRESENCE
AND EXPERIENCE HEAVEN ON EARTH*
Copyright © 2017 by Joseph Daratony

All rights reserved. No part of this publication may be reproduced, distributed, or transmitted in any form or by any means, including photocopying, recording, or other electronic or mechanical methods without the prior written permission of the publisher. For permission requests, solicit the publisher via the address below.

Scripture quotations marked KJV taken from the *Holy Bible*, King James Version.
Scripture quotations marked NKJV taken from the *New King James Version*. Copyright © 1979, 1980, 1982 by Thomas Nelson, Inc. Used by permission. All rights reserved.
Scripture quotations marked NLT are taken from the *Holy Bible*, New Living Translation, copyright © 1996, 2004. Used by permission of Tyndale House Publishers, Inc., Carol Stream, Illinois 60188. All rights reserved.
Scripture quotations marked NAS are taken from the *New American Standard Bible®*, Copyright © 1960, 1962, 1963, 1968, 1971, 1972, 1973, 1975, 1977, 1994 by The Lockman Foundation. Used by permission.
Scripture quotations marked NIV are taken from the *Holy Bible, New International Version®*, NIV®. Copyright © 1973, 1978, 1984, 2011 by Biblica, Inc.™ Used by permission of Zondervan. All rights reserved worldwide. www.zondervan.com. The "NIV" and "New International Version" are trademarks registered in the United States Patent and Trademark Office by Biblica, Inc.™
Scripture marked ISV taken from the Holy Bible: International Standard Version®. Copyright © 1996-forever by The ISV Foundation. ALL RIGHTS RESERVED INTERNATIONALLY. Used by permission.

Published by Mindstir Media LLC
45 Lafayette Rd. Suite 181 | North Hampton, NH 03862 | USA
1.800.767.0531 | www.mindstirmedia.com

Printed in the United States of America
ISBN-13: 978-0-9993872-8-3
Library of Congress Control Number: 2017954603

ACKNOWLEDGEMENTS

There are so many people to thank who have influenced my life. First, I have to thank my parents who raised my brothers and me in a strong Christian home. My mother and father are both very godly and love Jesus with all their hearts.

There have been pastors and leaders in the church who have also influenced me spiritually. Pastor Mark Freer of Grace Fellowship Church in Livonia, Michigan, was one of my first pastors. He is a very solid biblical teacher of the word. Also, Pastor Kim and Sheri Babcock who were pastors of Living Waters, in the Upper Peninsula of Michigan. They both had very powerful prophetic gifts and were very in tune with the Holy Spirit. They now serve as missionaries in Argentina.

Pastor Lee Cummings, lead pastor of Radiant Church in Richland, Michigan, exemplifies excellence in his ministry, with solid preaching of the word that was relevant, and his love for missions. I have to thank our present pastor, Nathaniel Redinger, who is the lead pastor of Life Point Community Church in Willow Springs, North Carolina. He is gifted in expository preaching and has a true heart of pastoring.

Last but not the least, I could have not come this far without my wife, Kathy, who keeps me grounded, and on the straight and narrow. She's the best godly mother anywhere having raised five children and one husband. I thank all my children who survived all my mistakes and did not rebel, and who are truly blessings from the Lord.

Of course, I continually thank God for His grace and the people He has put in my life as great influences.

CONTENTS

FOREWORD..15
INTRODUCTION..17
I Want to Live..17
    Staying Alive..17
    Living Heaven on Earth...18
    Beyond Goosebump Mountain..19
    God Is Not Playing Peek-A-Boo...20
    Activating the Spiritual GPS...20
    The Final Act...21
    God Says What?..22
CHAPTER ONE..23
Born-Again Atheist..23
    Show Me What You Believe...23
    The Great Divide...24
    Supernatural Atheist?..25
CHAPTER TWO..27
The Bermuda Tabernacle...27
    Open Highways, No More Road Blocks................................27
    God Wanted a House..28
    No More Bleacher Seats...29
    A Funny Thing Happened on the Journey..............................30
    Hide-and-Seek...31
    The General and the Manifest Presences of God....................31
    The Need for Navigation..31
    God Says What?..32

CHAPTER THREE 33
Ditch the Dogma 33
- Navigational Checkup 34
- Change in Plans 34
- Out of Sight Out of Mind 34
- There Is No Half Gospel 36
- God Says What? 36

CHAPTER FOUR 37
Supercharge Your Prayer Life 37
- The 90/10 Trap 37
- Intelligence Briefing 38
- Fake News Follies 38
- Spiritual Secrets 39
- The Secret that Led to a City Revival 39
- Secrets Vital to Evangelism 42
- God Says What? 43

CHAPTER FIVE 45
The Reality of the Supernatural World 45
- Understanding the Invisible Realm 46
- Two Worlds Tangle 47
- God's Address: Spirit Boulevard 47
- Beam Me up, Scotty 48
- God Says What? 49

CHAPTER SIX 51
The Presence-Driven Life 51
- Presence People 51
- Driving Options 52
- What About Bob? 53

Paralyzed Without the Presence..54
The X-Factor...55
Presence with a Punch..56
David Was Presence-Driven...57
God Says What?..58

CHAPTER SEVEN...59
Faith That You Can Sleep On..59
Impossible to Please God Without Faith.......................................60
Faith vs. Fear..60
Faith You Can Sleep On...62
God Says What?..63

CHAPTER EIGHT..65
Magnetic Desire..65
Magnetized Desire..65
Not Dead Yet!...66
Spiritual CPR..67
How Bad Do You Want It?...68
Enough of Dry-Eyed Desiring..69
God Does Not Play Games...70
Fast to Blast..70
How Much Are You Willing to Pay...71
The Secret Place Only Holds One..72
God Says What?..73

CHAPTER NINE..75
Revelation Revolution..75
The Power of Revelation..75
Apostle Paul's Prayer...78
The Spirit Realm Revealed...79

The Rhema and the Logos...80
God Says What?...83
CHAPTER TEN...85
Weapons of Mass Destruction...85
Find a Phone Booth...85
The Hidden Army of Giants..86
God's Favorite and Most-Used Phrase..................................87
The Weapon of the Word of God..88
The Weapon of Prayer...89
The Weapon of Worship..89
Can the Presence of God Be Detected in Your Life?...........90
The Power of His Presence Displayed..................................91
King David Knew the Power of His Presence.....................92
Guard the Presence of the Lord..93
God Says What?...94
CHAPTER ELEVEN..95
The Island of Misfits...95
What'sCrazy?..95
The Lord Is with You, Mighty Warrior................................96
What God Sees?...96
Warrior or Wimp...97
Life in the Spirit Is Easy, Life in the Flesh Is Hard............97
Am I Really Made for God Encounters?.............................97
God Has No Grandchildren Only Sons and Daughters—
Taking Ownership of Our Father's Kingdom.....................98
God Sees You as a Mighty Warrior......................................98
Everything Has a Purpose...99
You're in Good Company..99

 God Says What?..101

CHAPTER TWELVE..103
Escape the Matrix..103
 Does Your Thinking Need a Kicking?................................105
 Matrix Dreaming..106
 Separation, a Must...107
 How Deep Is the Rabbit Hole..108
 God Says What?..108

CHAPTER THIRTEEN..109
Life without Limits...109
 You Are More Than What You Have Done......................111
 God Wants Greater Works from Us..................................112
 Water the God Encounter Seed Within You.....................112
 Abraham Was a Sun Worshiper.......................................113
 A Blank Check..113
 God Says What?..114

CHAPTER FOURTEEN...115
Gushing Rivers or Dripping Faucets........................115
 Jump in, You Won't Drown...117
 Our Life Is Not a Log Ride in the Amusement Park.........118
 The Secret to the Secret Place...118
 Shadows Don't Heal..119
 God Says What?..119

CHAPTER FIFTEEN..121
Release God's Power..121
 Wait for My Power..122
 What Happens Without Power...122
 Thy Will Be Done on Earth, as It Is in Heaven.................123

- There Is No War or Enemy in Heaven..................124
- To Pray or Not to Pray..................125
- Authority vs. Prayer..................125
- Elijah's God Encounter..................126
- Dynamite Power..................127
- Dangerous Neglect..................128
- Jesus, Our Example..................129
- The Five Word Activation Question..................130
- The Gifts of the Spirit..................130
- Praying in the Spirit..................130
- Keep the Main Thing, the Main Thing..................131
- Unbroken Ministry..................132
- Jesus Doubles Down..................132
- The Church Is a Supernatural Entity..................133
- Only The Special and Few Can Do Miracles?..................133
- We All Like to Be Validated..................134

CHAPTER SIXTEEN..................135

Heavenly Minded and Earthly Good..................135
- Don't Throw The Baby Out with the Bathwater..................135
- Know the Mind of God..................136
- Naturally Supernatural..................136

FINAL THOUGHTS..................139
- A Life of Choices..................139
- A Life of Dependence..................139
- A Life of Manifesting..................140
- A Life of Grace..................140
- A Life of Training..................141

A Life of Challenge 141
ABOUT THE AUTHOR 143

FOREWORD

Do you often wonder about God and wish you could learn more about His presence? Do you desire to be in a place where you share rich intimacy with God? In this book, the author captures the step-by-step answers to the bogging questions in your heart. He shares his journey and how he came to a place of intimacy with God. There are so many misconceptions that were clearly addressed in this work. It takes you from a place of uncertainty into a place of knowing you can daily live in God's presence. The easy-to-read method used all through the book make it really captivating.

People often wish they can get to God through various means. They pray, yell, scream, and get into different modes to connect to the Almighty. As much as these may be able to quench certain longings in the soul, it may not be enough to enter into God's presence. The tranquility, peace, and joy that you desire is not in some far-fetched ideology. You can be in a prime position of joy and grandeur just as God designed it. Every shade of doubt, ignorance, and darkness has been cleared out of the way through this book.

When you find yourself asking questions such as: *Is there something more that I need to do in order to enjoy God's presence? Have I shut myself out of God's loving arms? Do I need to get into a secluded place in order to reach God?* you must understand that you hold in your hands a book that is going to be your worthy companion for many seasons. This is something that must be read and digested. Each of the gems that are outlined in this book will totally revolutionize your work with God. Do get in and find out answers to the issues in your heart.

John Paul
Senior Pastor, Real life Ministries

Ontario, Canada

INTRODUCTION

I Want to Live

Everybody wants to go to heaven, but nobody wants to die. Those words hit me like a ton of bricks while I was taking care of a patient in the emergency room. This patient asked me, "Am I going to live?"

I smiled and said, "Yes, you are."

He said, "Good. I want to live another ninety years." This guy was in his late sixties, so I did not think that was a possibility (not everyone could say that, but I was highly trained).

Talking to him, I learned he was a pastor of a church. I asked him, "Would you not rather be in heaven?"

He laughed, and that's when he responded, "Everyone wants to go to heaven, but nobody wants to die."

That is so true in our lives today. We all want to experience God and the blessing of God and heaven on earth, but we do not want to die. Every day, all our efforts are aimed at staying alive. We are groomed and trained that way at our very first breath, right out of the womb.

> We all want to experience God and the blessing of God and heaven on earth, but we do not want to die

Staying Alive

If you're old enough, you can remember the hit disco song by the Bee Gees, "Stayin' Alive," a popular song in the 70s. Can you imagine the church worship team singing that song for worship? I think there would be an outcry from the congregation; but in reality, that's what we do. I mean, we don't walk out from the church singing, "Ah, ah, ah, ah, stayin' alive, stayin' alive!" But our actions scream that song throughout the week. Scripture clearly teaches that the way to experience the presence of God is to put our flesh to death, which is the opposite of stayin'-alive doctrine. Please don't go to the bookstore and find an instruction book on how to leave this earth (that is not the death that I am talking about). Paul talks about dying to ourselves and letting the Spirit live through us. Remember, the fire does not come until the sacrifice is laid. The whole supernatural spirit realm is available to us. We can walk in the Spirit and live in the Spirit, and experience the presence of God on a daily basis in a mighty way. Why?

> We don't walk out from the church singing, "Ah, ah, ah, ah, stayin' alive, stayin' alive!" But our actions scream that song throughout the week

Because we are first, spiritual. That is our true self. However, we do not want to die and allow that to happen. We fight that because it is hard and painful, so much so that the Apostle Paul beat his body into subjection. What Paul meant was that he caused the flesh to suffer; he was not going around hitting himself. John the Baptist stated that He, meaning Jesus, must increase and he must decrease. That is our goal as Christians—to have the life of Jesus manifested and the presence of God manifested in our lives.

Living Heaven on Earth

The disciples asked Jesus to teach them to pray. Jesus in Matthew 6 says to them, "After this manner therefore pray ye: . . . Thy kingdom come, Thy will be done on earth as it is in heaven." (Matthew 6:9-10, KJV) That is a clear desire of our Father that His kingdom should rule in the world, this earth, while we are occupying it. Jesus did a whole lot more than dying for our sins, He came also preaching the kingdom of God and how we should experience it on earth in our lives.

There seems to be a brain freeze when it comes to God doing supernatural wonders in our midst and in today's world. People ask why that just does not happen. Those things have passed away. We don't need any miracles today. I believe in God without them. The excuses and reasoning go on and on. We have to grasp that with God there is no time variable; He is outside of time and space. God is always God and that never changes. He loves His children and will always seek a loving, intimate relationship with them. In fact, before the miracle of the cross, God's working with His people was limited to a select few. But today, because of the work of Christ, there are millions upon millions who can experience the supernatural and God's presence on a daily basis.

Jesus came so that we can experience heaven now; He brought the kingdom of God with Him. In Mark 1:15, Jesus said that the kingdom of God is at hand. He came preaching the kingdom; and if you want to see and experience the kingdom, you must be born again. In Luke 8:1, Jesus traveled around, preaching the good news of the kingdom. We do not have to wait until we enter heaven to enjoy the blessings of heaven. The bottom line is that we don't see or experience God because we see ourselves more and experience the world more rather than God. *Do not deceive yourself; you're right where you want to be in relation to God's presence.*

Beyond Goosebump Mountain

In our culture today, we are so stuffed with what the world offers, it leaves us with no hunger or desire for what God's presence offers. So we think that we have actually entered into the presence of God at church when a great song is sung, and we feel goosebumps. We conclude that surely the Lord was in this place. Hey, I feel goosebumps when I go into a walk in freezer, surely the Lord is in there also.

You may not realize it, but the one place you really want to be is abiding in the presence of God. We must go beyond God's general presence and right into His revealed presence—busting through all the man-made barriers that stop us from enjoying God's presence and kicking the door down. The only barriers to God's presence are man-made because God has no barriers to His presence. The pathway from His general presence into His revealed presence or manifested presence is one in which everyone says they want to travel and navigate, but few actually do.

> We must go beyond God's general presence and right into his revealed presence

Navigating God's presence is vital, and the map is laid out for us in the Bible. God gave us the map and said, "Seek Me, and if you seek Me with all your heart, you will find Me. When you find Me, you will experience more than goosebumps, you will experience My transforming, transporting, and tangible presence, and power." *We need to get to the place where it's not an effort to get into the secret place, but an effort to leave it.*

God Is Not Playing Peek-A-Boo

God's presence is a complicated subject, because God is complicated. I mean, who can really understand God? But one thing we know for sure is that not only is our joy full and complete in His presence (Psalm 16:11), but all of life and all ministry flow out of our relationship to His presence. Maybe at times, you feel like saying, "God, please show up and stay." The truth is He wants to, but when it comes right down to it, we don't want Him to show up and stay. No, God is not playing peek-a-boo, we actually are. Adam and Eve were the ones who hid from God's presence, not the other way around. True life is experienced from abiding and dwelling in His presence. Oh, sure, you can live life without experiencing God's presence and without experiencing heaven on earth, but it's not a life that will ever be truly fulfilled. "Unless the Lord builds the house those who labor are laboring in vain." *True joy and fulfillment are found in doing what you were created for—living in God's presence.*

> No, God is not playing peek-a-boo, we actually are

Activating the Spiritual GPS

We need to navigate from living in the general presence of God, which everyone does, to the manifested presence of God, which few experience. We need to set the destination on the GPS to the manifestation of God's presence. The destination of manifestation is the arrival point, and anything short of that is not the Lord's desired destination for us. We need to go from the outer court to the inner court, from knowledge to experience, and from being a spectator to a divine participant. God says that those who seek Him and seek Him with all their heart will find Him. We need to navigate because we need to seek and find. There are many things about God our finite minds cannot understand, like God being everywhere, and yet we still need to seek Him. It's just one of those truths.

> We need to go from the outer court to the inner court

The Final Act

In the beginning, God and man walked together. In the end, the presence of God with man will be restored. God has a plan, He has a goal, and He wants an intimate, personal, and explosive relationship with His children now and not later when we get to heaven.

I believe everything that happened throughout history in regards to God and His people leads to a relationship like the one He enjoyed with Adam and Eve before the Fall. The world began with a dynamic, uninterrupted relationship with the Father and His children, and I believe it will end that way. It can be that way right now because of what Jesus did for us on the cross.

In these last days, we will see and be part of an acceleration of the supernatural. We must be ready to flow in this movement and be positioned to be used by God in activating encounters with God to change this world. It has already begun, but for lack of better terms, it will be put on steroids and will exponentially explode in the church, and we must be ready and be part of it.

> In these last days, we will see and be part of an acceleration of the supernatural

I don't know about you, but I'm tired of hearing about God moving mightily with great encounters and power that are changing peoples' lives and not experiencing them myself. Don't get me wrong, I'm glad God is moving and showing up in the lives of people; but I'm desperate for God's presence in my own life, and I want to find the path into the very heart of His presence. If you're like me and want a heart-pounding, hair-raising, and ultimately full-of-joy experience with God, there's great news: He wants to give it to you in abundance. You, too, can have a steady dose of God encounters that will forever change your life and the world around you. *It's God's good pleasure to give you the kingdom.* This book cannot take you into God's presence or reveal God's presence to you, but it will navigate you in taking the right paths into His presence that will ignite your life in Christ. God desires for you to search for Him, to seek Him. This concept and truth are all throughout the Bible. But a lot of His children get lost on the way of searching and end up like those ships never to be found in the Bermuda Triangle.

God Says What?

There will be a "God Says What?" paragraph in some chapters. The Bible declares that everyone should prophesy. Let's not over-spiritualize this. Prophecy is just an expression and gift that articulates what God would be saying now or on a particular subject. So more than anything, what I want you to get from this book is an impartation of the presence of God. Knowledge and facts are secondary to me. So in the "God Says What?" segment, I will try to articulate what God would say.

God would say, So press on and don't give up, navigate, search, seek, and believe that I am there for you waiting to fellowship with you and manifest My presence in your life. I have given you the Holy Spirit to help in guiding you right to your destination, My presence. Be steadfast, unmovable, and always abounding in the work of the Lord and in expanding My kingdom.

CHAPTER ONE

Born-Again Atheist

They profess to know God, but by their deeds they deny Him, being detestable and disobedient, and worthless for any good deed.
(Titus 1:16, NAS)

No, I do not mean an atheist is literally born again. I'm referring to a declared Christian who says he is born again, but acts like an atheist. That does not even make sense, you might be thinking. How can you be a Christian and an atheist at the same time? Practical atheism is "holding an intellectual commitment to belief in God but thinking, feeling, and behaving as if there were no God." What is the difference between an atheist who does not obey God and a person who says they are a Christian and does not obey God? One is a stated atheist and the other a practical atheist. Our navigation path must begin with a practice and action that speaks of God as being real and that our beliefs are not in word only, but in actions. The church today, as a whole, lives as if God does not exist and wonders why they are not experiencing God in supernatural ways. The Bible strongly declares the kingdom of God is not in word, but in power. Again, that power in Greek means supernatural power.

> Practical atheism is "holding an intellectual commitment to belief in God but thinking, feeling, and behaving as if there were no God."

Show Me What You Believe

Craig Groeschel recounted the famous Charles Blondin (the first to cross Niagara Falls on a tightrope) as he once walked across Niagara Falls pushing a wheelbarrow. The story goes that an exuberant onlooker called out, "You could cross with a man in that wheelbarrow!" Blondin agreed and invited the man to be his "passenger," but the man nervously declined the invitation. To this, Groeschel commented:

> My dysfunctional relationship with God was often like that. I've always believed in God, just not enough to trust Him with my whole life in His wheelbarrow. I knew God could fulfill His promises, but I was never sure He'd do it for me. My selfish Christian Atheist view was that God existed for me, rather than I for Him. If He'd do what I thought He should, I'd trust Him more. If He'd come through for me, I'd give Him more of my life. If He made my life better and pain-free, I'd believe Him more passionately. But anytime God didn't meet my expectations, we had a problem. God created me in His image. I returned the favor and created Him in mine. The kind of God I wanted to believe in was this: if He's not what I want, then He can't have my whole life[1].

In the book of Titus, chapter one, this is what Paul is describing. We say a lot of things, but our life is saying something else. In other words, your life is shouting too loudly. I can't hear what you're saying.

The Great Divide

We need to navigate roads that would lead us to or away from experiencing God's manifested presence. For instance, we need to choose between the road of religion or relationship; fear or faith; knowledge or revelation; petition or command; bad dogma or sound doctrine; intentions or desire; the visible or the invisible; and the outer court or the inner court. No doubt, there is a gap between the potential of the church and the current output or results of the church.

> No doubt, there is a gap between the potential of the church and the current output or results of the church

[1] Craig Groeschel, *The Christian Atheist*, (Grand Rapids, Michigan: Zondervan, 2010), p.233-4.

After about two thousand years of existence, with the power of Almighty God at our disposal, about forty percent of the world has not been reached or even heard of the Gospel. The church has lost its way into the manifested presence of God. We need to recalibrate our spiritual GPS and get back on course. The church is in desperate need of the presence of God, and in these final days that are remaining, there's going to be a showdown of the two kingdoms and we need to move in the power and presence of God like never before.

Supernatural Atheist?

Okay, maybe it's been a little harsh so far. Let's say Christians are Christians no matter if they act like God does not exist. At least they proclaim there is a God and confess that Jesus is the Son of God. So what if they don't act like God's presence is right there with them and don't obey or please God? Hey, they are forgiven, and life goes on. Maybe we can just narrow the atheist part to their believing in the supernatural power of God working in our lives today in signs, wonders, miracles, healing and so on. Granted, there are millions of wonderful children of God who say and believe the supernatural and God manifesting Himself was in the past and for a purpose.

They are still part of the church and going to heaven. Paul, on the other hand, did not believe that at all. In fact, he wrote, "My message and my preaching were not with wise and persuasive words, but with a demonstration of the Spirit's power, so that your faith might not rest on men's wisdom, but on God's power." (1 Corinthians 2:4, NAS) What was Paul saying and what does he mean? He could have reasoned with them. The Corinthians loved that the religious leaders of that city engaged themselves in philosophical discussions. Paul was well-trained in that sort of debate. But he avoided that and said, "I want to come in power." The demonstration of the Spirit and of power is the manifestation of the Holy Spirit in signs, wonders, miracles and the other gifts of the Holy Spirit. The demonstration of power (the power of the Holy Ghost) is in the manifestation and demonstration of the power gifts of the Holy Spirit. The demonstration of the Spirit is in the manifestation of the word of wisdom, the word of knowledge, discerning of spirits, prophecy, diverse kinds of tongues, interpretation of tongues and other spiritual manifestations.

> The gospel or the Word of God is not supposed to
> go forth in word only, but it is to be accompanied
> by the demonstration of the Spirit and of power.

It is through the greatness of God's power that His enemies will submit to Him. We cannot afford to be supernatural atheists. We have to navigate and find our way into the very presence of God and live the gospel, not just read it.

CHAPTER TWO

The Bermuda Tabernacle

Therefore, brothers, since we have confidence to enter the Most Holy Place by the blood of Jesus, by a new and living way opened for us through the curtain, that is, His body . . . let us draw near to God with a sincere heart in full assurance of faith."
(Hebrews 10:19–22, NIV)

Notice the word *confidence* mentioned by the writer of Hebrews. At one time, men and priests would die if they entered the Holy Place unprepared, so naturally, there would be some anxiety involved in the process of entering God's presence. Even if you covered all your bases, you always thought, "What if I missed something?" Wow. God took His presence seriously and we should, too. But, the writer of this verse says now we can enter in with confidence. No one dies, and in fact, he goes on to say enter in boldly. That is quite different from before Christ's time.

Open Highways, No More Road Blocks

According to the Scripture above, everything has changed in regards to the presence of God from before the cross to after the cross. There is a new way and a better way to navigate into the presence of God because of the blood of Jesus. There is a new and living way into God presence, unlike the old curtain and the old veil that separated us from the presence of God. But to the disappointment of God, many of us get lost going from God's general presence and finding our way into His manifested presence, much like the ships and planes that travel through the Bermuda Triangle.

The Bermuda Triangle, also known as the Devil's Triangle, is a section of the Atlantic Ocean roughly bounded by Miami, Bermuda, and Puerto Rico, where dozens of ships and airplanes have disappeared. Unexplained circumstances surround some of these accidents, including one in which the pilots of a squadron of US Navy bombers became disoriented while flying over the area; the planes were never found. Other boats and planes have seemingly vanished from the area in good weather without even radioing distress messages. To bring this story home to what we are talking about, navigating the presence of God, many Christians are getting lost in the outer court of the tabernacle and are disappearing from navigating to the manifest presence of God.

God Wanted a House

After God delivered the people from the bondage of the Egyptians, He desired to live among them. So much so that He instructed Moses to build Him a house in which He could dwell. "Have the people of Israel build Me a holy sanctuary so I can live among them." (Exodus 25:8, NLT)

In the story of Moses and the tabernacle that God told Him to build, we see the beginning of God reaching out and trying to teach His children about His presence. We need to stop and think about that request by God, that God wanted to dwell with His people and manifest His presence. More than anything else, the tabernacle was God's dwelling place among His people. Of course, God did not literally live there as people live in their houses. God cannot be contained in any building, however grand. But the tabernacle signified the presence of God in Israel. God manifested Himself and said, "I am with you." Therefore, the tabernacle, and later the temple, were crucial to the Israelites because they signified God's presence.

The tabernacle was to be made up of three parts. The outer court, the inner court, and the Holy of Holies. It was the purpose of God to reveal some aspects of His presence to His children through the construction of the tabernacle. He wanted us to understand that there is the general presence of God, which was represented in the outer court. Also, there was the inner court which represented His manifested presence, the place in which God dwelt. A very important veil existed between the two courts that separated them. This was to prevent unauthorized people from entering the inner court where God's presence dwelt. The word "veil" in Hebrew means a screen, divider or separator that hides. What was this curtain hiding? Essentially, it was shielding sinful man from a holy God. Whoever entered into the Holy of Holies was entering the very presence of God. In fact, anyone except the high priest who entered the Holy of Holies would die. Even the high priest, God's chosen mediator with His people, could only pass through the veil and enter this sacred dwelling once a year on a prescribed day called the Day of Atonement.

No More Bleacher Seats

Because of what Jesus did for us on the cross, the barrier that separated the Holy Place and the Holy of Holies has been destroyed. As mentioned before, at one time, only the high priest was allowed into the Holy of Holies. Everyone else had bleacher seats, so to speak, in the nosebleed section. Have you ever been to a game or play where you were so far removed from the action everyone looked like ants? *Well as far as God is concerned, everyone now can be part of the action instead of just being spectators.* Jesus has made available to us front-row premier box seats in the purposes and activity of God.

> Well as far as God is concerned, everyone now can be part of the action instead of just being spectators

If you or a church only acknowledges the general presence of God and does not experience His revealed, manifested presence, then that will lead to a dead, boring church or a difficult life for you. How can I say that? I cannot, but the Bible does. In the book of Revelation, John refers to the church of Sardis as being dead. "To the angel of the church in Sardis write: These are the words of him who holds the seven spirits of God and the seven stars. I know your deeds; you have a reputation of being alive, but you are dead."

That is a scary thought. Of course, the presence of God was there, in the general sense, but not in a manifested way where people were having encounters with Him. They had a head knowledge of God and knew of Him, but they did not know Him.

> "'Am I only a God nearby, declares the Lord, and not a God far away? Who can hide in secret places so that I cannot see them?" declares the Lord. Do not I fill heaven and earth?' declares the Lord."
> (Jeremiah 23:23–24, NIV)

Theologically, we know that God is omnipresent, but that fact is not discerned with the senses. It is a reality, but that reality may not seem relevant to the majority of people on the planet who have no sense of His presence. Just like Jacob stated, "God was in this place, and I did not know it." The majority of people believe He is distant, not close, and that feeling becomes their perceived reality. I can hear some people saying, "If God wants to reveal Himself in my life or anyone else's, He will." This statement is true. He could reveal Himself, but God has chosen to expand His kingdom a different way. His method is to use His children who absolutely desire and seek His manifested presence.

A Funny Thing Happened on the Journey

In Matthew 27:51, it says, "At that moment the curtain of the temple was torn in two from top to bottom. The earth shook, the rocks split." (NIV) We, as a church and as God's children, have complete access to His presence. Our journey is unhindered going from the outer court to the Holy of Holies, where God's manifested presence is. But a strange thing is happening for a lot of people; they disappear like the ships and planes in the Bermuda Triangle. It's like they get sucked into a black hole never to come out. But it's sad in the church today. Most of the church is lost and not to be found in the inner court; they are wandering in the outer court or completely off the grid. They feel content just playing church and not really being transported into His presence or having the Lord reveal His presence to them. They don't realize that they can escape the outer court; or if they do realize they can escape, they give it no thought. Maybe their love for this rock is more important than being transported into the His presence. They do not realize that God has invited them into His manifested presence. We say, in regards to the Israelites, that they were stupid for wandering in the desert for forty years. But, in fact, a lot of us are doing the same thing. We are playing at the outer court, we are wandering this planet, when *our true purpose is in the Holy of Holies; our true purpose in is the presence of God.* Our true purpose is abiding in Him, in His secret place.

Hide-and-Seek

Another way to describe this complex theme of God's presence and to illustrate the difference between His general presence and His manifested presence is with the hide-and-seek game. I'm sure you have played hide-and-seek at some point in your lifetime. I remember playing as a child with my father and brothers. My father would go into a room and hide, and of course, we would search for him. We could not see him, feel him, or hear him, but we knew that his presence was there. Finally, we would find him, and he would reveal his presence to us. In other words, his presence manifested. He showed himself. That game illustrates God's general presence and God's manifested presence perfectly. *God chooses to show up at times, and when He does, a God encounter happened.*

> God chooses to show up at times and when He does, a God encounter happened

The General and the Manifest Presences of God

Both the general and the manifest have benefits in our lives. When a person has a revelation of the general presence, he or she will excel in character and holiness. Think about it, if you're truly aware of the presence of God being everywhere which includes where you are, you will do what pleases God even when you're alone. That is character—doing the right thing when no one is watching. Also, it leads to a more holy life being aware of God's presence everywhere. But the manifest presence offers intimacy, power, and experience with God and encountering the supernatural. Both are important, and both needed, but many stop at the general experience and do not enter His manifest experience.

The Need for Navigation

Experiencing God's presence just does not happen unless He sovereignly intervenes in our life. But for the most part, God has said to seek Him, find Him, hunger for Him, and desperately navigate through all the hindrances into His presence and you will be rewarded.

God is always communicating with you. However, like Adam and Eve, we may be hiding. After Adam and Eve sinned, they hid themselves from the presence of the Lord. The same thought came to the children of Israel after being delivered from Egypt. They approached Moses and said to him, "You go before God for us. We do not want to see Him." They were hiding, and they were afraid. God was calling and they were just like those ships that disappeared in the Bermuda Triangle. People who hide from God are lost. Sometimes, we are the same way, and at other times, we are just not in tune or looking for where God is working or what God is doing in people around us. In other words, we are not in the zone. If you can recognize what God is doing around you in your everyday life, it will be so much easier for you to experience God. We will explore that area later on how to recognize what God is up to. My prayer as you continue in this book is that God would bring you to the point that you regularly encountering him and being transported into His presence. We walk in His manifested presence, not His general presence.

God Says What?

God would say, "The veil has been destroyed, and the invitation has been spoken. Come boldly into My throne room and experience My presence. I desire to dwell with you and My passion for you is great. Don't stop seeking, for your desire draws My presence to you as your desire draws you to Me."

CHAPTER THREE

Ditch the Dogma

Ye men of Israel, hear these words; Jesus of Nazareth, a man approved of God among you by miracles and wonders and signs, which God did by Him in the midst of you, as ye yourselves also know.
(Acts 2:22, KJV)

In this verse, Peter is preaching to men in Israel. He states that Jesus was a man who was approved by God with mighty works. Why did he say man and not God who was approved by God? These mighty works could only be done by God. These supernatural works testified that God was with Him. Why did Jesus need this validation and we don't? How can we say we can do the work of making disciples and neglect the validation and proof that God is with us? Are we better than Jesus and do not need the supernatural work of the Spirit in our lives as He did?

Sometimes, our thinking needs a kicking. That's the way it was for John the Baptist. Although he already baptized Jesus in the Jordan River, in prison, he was having doubts. He sent his disciples to ask Jesus if He really is the one. "Then, Jesus, answering said unto them, 'Go your way, and tell John what things ye have seen and heard; how that the blind see, the lame walk, the lepers are cleansed, the deaf hear, the dead are raised, to the poor the gospel is preached'" (Luke 7:22, KJV).

> Sometimes, our thinking needs a kicking

Jesus highlighted the supernatural activities in His life. He pointed out the works of God in His life. That is what separated Him from the religious elite. That is what separated Him from the world. It is no different for you today. The things we need to point to is the work of His divine presence. The world can mimic the church in everything except the presence of the God being manifested in our lives. This belief that only Jesus and only a few select others in His day could have done those miracles and supernatural wonders is the surest way into the Bermuda Triangle.

Navigational Checkup

The Apostle Paul says we should examine our faith. We should check and make sure we are on the right navigational longitude and latitude. This is so vital that we make sure our belief and doctrine are correct. Listen to the warning to one of the seven churches in the book of revelations, Jesus says,

> But I say to the rest of you in Thyatira, who do not hold to her teaching and have not learned the so-called deep things of Satan: I will place no further burden upon you. Nevertheless, hold fast to what you have until I come. And to the one who is victorious and continues in My work until the end, I will give authority over the nations. (Revelation 2:24-26, NIV)

Today I run into many Christians with very strange beliefs that I cannot even get my head around. Jesus is our example, and He is the same yesterday, today, and forever. He does not change.

Change in Plans

Imagine Jesus saying, "I am going to adjust the rules and plans a little. For My life, and maybe about thirty to forty years after My death, we will go with the miracles signs and wonders plan. After that, we will adjust, and I'm going to pull out the supernatural works from the church, and you will have to evangelize the whole world just by your preaching." Sounds kind of silly, but millions of God's children believe that's what happened. Either you're going to have to believe Jesus when He said, "the works that I do you will do also and greater works you will do," or you're not going to believe Him. That was not just for the disciples of that time because we know of several other people flowing in the supernatural after Jesus ascended to heaven.

Out of Sight Out of Mind

It is a major mistake to solidify your doctrine and beliefs on what you see and experience in your life. On the same note, it is just as bad to believe in doctrine because of what you don't see and experience. I don't believe miracles or the supernatural are for today, because I never experienced anything like that or observed any activity of that sort. Therefore, I have to conclude that miracles, signs and wonders, and experiencing the presence of God in a supernatural way are not for this lifetime. With that attitude, you have just left the path to experiencing God's presence and have raised major problems in many statements that Jesus made in regards to bringing His kingdom to earth.

We discussed earlier how a funny thing happened on the way to the Holy of Holies. One major thing is that we have an enemy that will do whatever it takes to keep us from experiencing God's presence and releasing His presence into the world in supernatural works. Satan cannot stop you from being born again and being saved from your sins. He cannot stop you from entering into heaven after you leave this earth. But he can hinder you in your relationship with God, and he can bring confusion and deception and blind the minds of some. In the book of John, it says the devil comes to kill, steal and destroy. He does not like God's children very much. He wants to kill you, and he will try.

Sure, he says, go to church and worship, just do not experience His presence that will bring the supernatural. Sure, read your Bible, but do not get revelation. I will not like that. Go ahead and quote the Scripture, just do not really believe it. This scenario is just like Pharaoh when he said to Moses and the Israelites, "Well, okay, you can leave but only go so far." And Pharaoh said, "I will let you go that you may sacrifice to the Lord your God in the wilderness; only you shall not go very far away: entreat for me" (Exodus 8:28, KJV). Gee, thank you, mighty Pharaoh, that is really swell of you. That was not the reply from Moses, and that should not be our reply when it comes to honoring God and continuing His work on earth and expanding His kingdom.

> "And Pharaoh said, I will let you go that you may sacrifice to the Lord your God in the wilderness; only you shall not go very far away: entreat for me" (Exodus 8:28)

There Is No Half Gospel

Can you imagine going into church and saying to your pastor, "Please can I just get half the sermon today?" (Although in many cases that might not be a bad thing.) Or going to the worship leader and saying, "Just sing a half of a song." No one wants a portion of the gospel. They want the full good news, and they deserve the full good news. Like the late newscaster Paul Harvey used to say, "Here's the rest of the story." Well, the rest of the story is displaying the supernatural presence of God into this world with mighty signs and wonders confirming His existence.

"Through mighty signs and wonders, by the power of the Spirit of God; so that from Jerusalem, and round about unto Illyricum, I have fully preached the gospel of Christ" (Romans 15:19, KJV). The good news of the gospel is not only that we have salvation from our sins but also the kingdom of God has come, and because of what Christ did for us on the cross, the original plan of God has been restored. Right before Jesus left this earth, His words were that all authority has been given to Me, therefore go and do what I did. Preaching the full gospel with great and mighty signs following. This is hard to say, but if the signs and the supernatural are not following you and showing up in your life, are you really preaching the good news the way God desires you to?

God Says What?

> God would say, "Do not put Me in a box. I am the same yesterday, today, and forever, I do not change. I am supernatural, and everything I do is supernatural. Why be so surprised by the supernatural? Believe the supernatural to become natural in your life. That is the only way My kingdom will grow, and the works of the devil will be destroyed. Your battle is with the spiritual realm, so what you do must be in the spiritual realm or supernatural."

CHAPTER FOUR

Supercharge Your Prayer Life

*But they that wait upon the Lord shall renew their
strength; they shall mount up with wings as eagles;
they shall run, and not be weary; and they shall walk,
and not faint.*
(Isaiah 40:31, KJV)

I was going to name this chapter "Pray Less and Experience God More," but I thought that would offend some people.

Before you get upset and get a refund on this book, just hear me out. I don't know about you, but when I'm quiet before the Lord in my alone time, sometimes, I just want to keep on talking and praying. I can imagine God the Father turning to Jesus and saying, "Is he done yet?"

The 90/10 Trap

From my experience and attending prayer meetings, ninety percent of the time is making requests and petitions to the Lord. Or in our time alone with God, it's probably the same for most people that we do most of the talking. I can just hear the Father say, "Good, they are done talking. Now I can get in a couple of words." At that point, we get up and pat ourselves on the back because we fulfilled our duty of praying. We give no chance for the Holy Spirit to speak to us, and we give ourselves no chance in hearing the still, quiet voice.

It's hard just to sit in quiet and train ourselves to hear the Spirit. We should reverse the trap: listen ninety percent of the time and speak ten percent. After all, it's us who need the leading of God in our lives. He does not need our guidance. But He does want our heart and our intimate fellowship with Him. Prayer is communication, not an hour's speech we give to God. In NAS, the word most often translated "wait" in the sense of waiting on the Lord is the Hebrew *qavah*. *Qavah* means (1) "to bind together" (perhaps by twisting strands as in making a rope), (2) "look patiently," (3) "tarry or wait," and (4) "hope, expect, look eagerly. The binding together is awesome.

That's how we become strong, by being bound to the presence of God. Jesus referred to this when He said, "If you abide in Me and I in you, great things will happen." He also went on to say, "If you are abiding in Me, ask whatever you want, and it shall be done for you." That is a great promise and something that should be used in our lives a lot more. But keep in mind the most important thing we can do is wait and soak in His presence. It does not take long to make our requests to God.

> **Prayer is communication, not an hour's speech we give to God.**

Intelligence Briefing

The President's Daily Brief (PDB) is a top-secret document produced and given each morning at seven forty-five to the president of the United States. This is the time the president gets all the top secrets from the FBI and the CIA and all the other agencies that can shed light on what is happening in the world, so the president can make more informed decisions and not shoot in the dark. This is one thing the government does well. I have been in the medical field for a while, and we have teams that are assigned to a patient. We all share our findings and come up with a plan of action that is on purpose, so we are not just shooting blindly.

Fake News Follies

It is fascinating to observe the rise of fake news popping up from major news networks. Almost every week, you hear a news network recant and apologize for a misleading story. It's becoming more difficult to know what is true, and what not to believe.

For most of the world, and that includes the church, the first choice of news and information is major networks. There are many—CBS, ABC, CNN, FOX, MSNBC and many more.

The key to Jesus's ministry and success is that He made it a priority to break away and tune into the heavenly broadcasting network. Imagine a heavenly news organization called Throne Room Connections. The owner of the station is God the Father. His main program is the *Rhema*—Revelation Show. It's a continuous broadcast of up-to-date kingdom happenings.

The chief correspondent is none other than the Holy Spirit Himself, who brings you breaking news delivered directly into your heart, with unbiased reporting, and uninterrupted, commercial-free streaming. It's guaranteed true news, and zero chance of being misleading.

The point is, we need to hear from God ourselves. Jesus made it a practice to break away and tune into the broadcasting which comes from heaven. This must become our practice as the church. God is continually speaking to us, but we are not tuning into the right frequency. Our Father wants to reveal secrets to us so that we can become more effective in expanding His kingdom and more effective in our life and ministry.

Spiritual Secrets

The church needs to be smart and rely on secrets and intelligence from the Holy Spirit. "And He who searches our hearts knows the mind of the Spirit, because the Spirit intercedes for God's people in accordance with the will of God" (Romans 8:27, NIV). "The secret of the LORD is with them that fear Him; and He will shew them His covenant" (Psalm 25:14, KJV). Also, Jesus says, "Henceforth I call you not servants; for the servant knoweth not what his lord doeth: but I have called you friends; for all things that I have heard of My Father I have made known unto you" (John 15:15, KJV). The Lord desires to reveal secrets to us so we will not be shooting blindly. We are engaged in a spiritual war. We must see what we are up against. That's why Paul's greatest prayer was for believers' eyes to be enlightened, so they would see into the Spirit and understand the tactics of the devil. Jesus, many times, revealed secrets, and the end result was revival and many healings and deliverances.

The Secret that Led to a City Revival

Jesus knew the Pharisees had heard that He was baptizing and making more disciples than John (though Jesus Himself didn't baptize them, His disciples did). So He left Judea and returned to Galilee.

He had to go through Samaria on the way. Eventually He came to the Samaritan village of Sychar, near the field that Jacob gave to his son

Joseph. Jacob's well was there; and Jesus, tired from the long walk, sat wearily beside the well about noontime. Soon a Samaritan woman came to draw water, and Jesus said to her, "Please give Me a drink." He was alone at the time because His disciples had gone into the village to buy some food.

The woman was surprised, for Jews refuse to have anything to do with Samaritans. She said to Jesus, "You are a Jew, and I am a Samaritan woman. Why are You asking me for a drink?"

Jesus replied, "If you only knew the gift God has for you and who you are speaking to, you would ask Me, and I would give you living water."

"But Sir, You don't have a rope or a bucket," she said, "and this well is very deep.

Where would You get this living water? And besides, do You think You're greater than our ancestor Jacob, who gave us this well? How can You offer better water than he and his sons and his animals enjoyed?"

Jesus replied, "Anyone who drinks this water will soon become thirsty again. But those who drink the water I give will never be thirsty again. It becomes a fresh, bubbling spring within them, giving them eternal life."

"Please, Sir," the woman said, "give me this water! Then I'll never be thirsty again, and I won't have to come here to get water."

"Go and get your husband," Jesus told her.

"I don't have a husband," the woman replied.

Jesus said, "You're right! You don't have a husband—for you have had five husbands, and you aren't even married to the man you're living with now. You certainly spoke the truth!"

"Sir," the woman said, "You must be a prophet. So tell me, why is it that you Jews insist that

> Jerusalem is the only place of worship, while we Samaritans claim it is here at Mount Gerizim, where our ancestors worshiped?"
>
> Jesus replied, "Believe Me, dear woman, the time is coming when it will no longer matter whether you worship the Father on this mountain or in Jerusalem. You Samaritans know very little about the one you worship, while we Jews know all about Him, for salvation comes through the Jews. But the time is coming—indeed it's here now—when true worshipers will worship the Father in spirit and in truth. The Father is looking for those who will worship Him that way. For God is Spirit, so those who worship Him must worship in spirit and in truth."
>
> The woman said, "I know the Messiah is coming—the one who is called Christ. When He comes, He will explain everything to us."
>
> Then Jesus told her, "I am the Messiah!"
>
> Just then His disciples came back. They were shocked to find Him talking to a woman, but none of them had the nerve to ask, "What do You want with her?" or "Why are You talking to her?" The woman left her water jar beside the well and ran back to the village, telling everyone, "Come and see a man who told me everything I ever did! Could He possibly be the Messiah?" So the people came streaming from the village to see Him.
> (John 4:1–30, NLT)

It is important to state that Jesus did not know these secrets because He was God. Jesus stated in a couple of places He willingly laid down His divinity and only did things in the power and by the power of the Holy Spirit. This is a very important biblical truth that Jesus could do nothing by Himself, but only what was revealed to Him by the Father. This truth allows us to do the works Jesus said He wanted us to do—supernatural works. If Jesus performed anything supernaturally by His divine nature, that would take all responsibility from us and give us an excuse of saying, "Well, He was God."

Secrets Vital to Evangelism

Jesus revealed to the woman at least two secrets that would only be known from an intel report that was given to Him. First, that the woman had five husbands. Second, that the one she was with now was not her husband. These pieces of knowledge captured the attention of the woman and probably frightened her. When you read someone's secret mail, that definitely grabs their attention.

> **If Jesus performed anything supernaturally by His divine nature, that would take all responsibility from us and give us an excuse of saying, "Well, He was God."**

There are many examples recorded in the Scripture, and this next secret was revealed by an angel to Phillip, and the end result was the salvation of the Ethiopian.

> Now an angel of the Lord spoke to Philip, saying, "Arise and go toward the south along the road which goes down from Jerusalem to Gaza." This is desert. So he arose and went. And behold, a man of Ethiopia, a eunuch of great authority under Candace the queen of the Ethiopians, who had charge of all her treasury and had come to Jerusalem to worship was returning. And sitting in his chariot, he was reading Isaiah the prophet. Then the Spirit said to Philip, "Go near and overtake this chariot."
>
> So Philip ran to him, and heard him reading the prophet Isaiah, and said, "Do you understand what you are reading?"
>
> And he said, "How can I, unless someone guides me?" And he asked Philip to come up and sit with him. The place in the Scripture which he read was this:
>
> "He was led as a sheep to the slaughter;
> And as a lamb before its shearer is silent, So He opened not His mouth. In His humiliation His

justice was taken away. And who will declare His generation? For His life is taken from the earth."

So the eunuch answered Philip and said, "I ask you, of whom does the prophet say this, of himself or of some other man?" Then Philip opened his mouth, and beginning at this Scripture, preached Jesus to him. Now as they went down the road, they came to some water. And the eunuch said, "See, here is water. What hinders me from being baptized?"

Then Philip said, "If you believe with all your heart, you may."

And he answered and said, "I believe that Jesus Christ is the Son of God."

So he commanded the chariot to stand still. And both Philip and the eunuch went down into the water, and he baptized him. Now when they came up out of the water, the Spirit of the Lord caught Philip away, so that the eunuch saw him no more; and he went on his way rejoicing. But Philip was found at Azotus. And passing through, he preached in all the cities till he came to Caesarea. (Acts 8:26-40, NKJV).

Because of these secrets being revealed, evangelism is more effective, and we who are involved are not shooting in the dark blindly and have much greater results.

God Says What?

God would say, "When I said I will not leave you alone, I was not lying. We are partners, and I will reveal all things to you if you open your ears and listen.

In the stillness, I will speak. In the quiet, I will reveal so that you will know the operation and the strongholds of our enemy. Too often my children go at it

> Because of these secrets being revealed, evangelism is more effective and we who are involved are not shooting in the dark blindly and have much greater results.

alone and too often very little happens. Be patient, be still, and allow My leading and revelation direct your paths."

CHAPTER FIVE

The Reality of the Supernatural World

> I know a man in Christ who fourteen years ago was caught up to the third heaven. Whether it was in the body or out of the body I do not know—God knows. And I know that this man—whether in the body or apart from the body I do not know, but God knows—was caught up to paradise and heard inexpressible things, things that no one is permitted to tell.
> (2 Corinthians 12:2–4, NIV)

This verse puts the *Twilight Zone* to shame. People in today's world are fascinated with the supernatural, and the church seems to be the opposite. Most say stay away from things like witchcraft and new age. Well, someone forgot to tell the Apostle Paul he should not experience things like that, and especially write about things like that. It's very uncomfortable. Wake up, church! We are in a reality, not a *Twilight Zone* episode, that will continue until Jesus comes back.

In chapter two of the book of Ephesians, Paul writes, You were in the kingdom of darkness. You've been ransomed. Now you're in the Kingdom of His beloved Son. There's this new entity called the church. And it's been a mystery, but it's been in the mind and the heart of God since eternity—Jew, Gentile, one new thing, new relationship. Paul was explaining to the church about the two different worlds, the physical and the spiritual.

> Wake up, church! We are in a reality twilight episode that will continue until Jesus comes back

Favorite movies, books and heroes in our culture reveal a fascination with the supernatural. We are drawn to the idea of power and the supernatural. I think it is because we are spiritual beings first and then physical, but the world does not know it. This is not a negative desire at all, but the enemy wants to exploit this hunger and use it to enslave us with a false power.

This makes learning about the Holy Spirit and how He functions even more important.

We want to be wise and discerning so we can recognize when something is God and when something is counterfeit. We want to be people who know and demonstrate the true power of God's Spirit so others can know Him and experience His power also. Bill Johnson said we as Christians "owe the world an encounter with God," and any encounter with God is going to be a power encounter and a supernatural encounter.

Understanding the Invisible Realm

We read a lot in the Bible about the unseen realm, but we have a hard time understanding how to actually relate to it. What do we understand about "heavenly places?" (Ephesians 2:6). Paul refers to the third heaven. If there is a third heaven, there is a second heaven also. How do we tap into "the powers of the age to come and the kingdom of God?" (Hebrews 6:5). How do we understand the principalities and powers described by the Apostle Paul in the book of Ephesians? What do we understand about demons and spirits? Why did it take Michael the archangel to battle twenty-one days to get Daniel an answer? How do we see the relationship of angels, good and bad, with us and the nations? And what about the role of, and our relationship with, the person of the Holy Spirit? What about hell? And paradise? When Jesus came, He did so much more than die on the cross. He also brought the kingdom to be re-established here on earth.

> When Jesus came, he did so much more than to die on the cross.

Heaven, then, is not so much a place to go or a place related to a future, post-death experience, but is more of a description of a position or dimension of power, authority and reality that affects the affairs of humanity on earth. It is the place, or dimension, where the will of God is being done in all its fullness without the presence of evil. This is what we are praying to manifest on earth. We are to enforce the work that Jesus did on the cross. Jesus came to destroy the works of the devil. We are also commissioned with authority and power to destroy the works of the devil.

Two Worlds Tangle

In the beginning, God created the heavens and the earth. This was not just earth and sky. "The heavens" is the biblical name for the spiritual world that exists in parallel to the physical world. God created a multidimensional universe. We can only see the three dimensions of physical space, plus time so we assume that is all that exists. The spiritual world consists of many more dimensions of reality beyond what we can see. The spiritual world is more real than the physical because the spiritual realm is eternal.

Jesus's mission was to bring His kingdom and its power to the earth, to rescue men and women that were in bondage to the kingdom of darkness and set them free. Experiencing heaven on earth is what we need to aspire to. That was the way Jesus walked. That is the way we are called to walk this earth.

> I say, walk by the Spirit, and you will not carry out the desire of the flesh. For the flesh sets its desire against the Spirit, and the Spirit against the flesh; for these are in opposition to one another, so that you may not do the things that you please. (Galatians 5:16–17, NAS)

God's Address: Spirit Boulevard

I hope you like traveling because our journey in navigating God's presence, it is going to require a cross-dimensional trek. For the most part, we experience God by the work of the Holy Spirit transporting us into His presence. What I mean is, our spirit is abiding in God's presence. That happens many ways, sometimes being transported into His presence, and at other times, God revealing Himself to us with a strong presence. Still others experience God in dreams and visions, and the list goes on and on because God is a creative God. For instance, as Israel was departing Egypt, God manifested Himself as a cloud by day and a fire by night. God can manifest Himself to us through angels, signs and wonders. He can also take us into spirit realms as we are transported as the Apostle Paul was several times. Many of God's children have experienced being taken into the spiritual realms, like Isaiah, Ezekiel, Stephen and many more.

Beam Me up, Scotty

Sometimes, Hollywood creates TV shows or movies that reveal real spiritual truths that can explain deep theology in a simple way. *Star Trek* with Captain James Kirk and his starship *Enterprise* is an excellent example of some deep theology.

Imagine for a moment that the starship *Enterprise* of *Star Trek* is the presence of God. Going further, imagine Scotty, who is usually the guy who beams people up and down to different planets and locations, is the Holy Spirit. Now, we get to you. Imagine you are stuck on a far-off planet about to be destroyed by an alien force. You take your communicator, press it and tell Scotty to beam you up to the *Enterprise*. That is an illustration of what it means to experience the manifested or the revealed presence of God. We can't just go to where the *Enterprise* is; we must be transported into it and to experience the reality of it. The *Enterprise* must in some way reveal itself or transport you into it.

For most of the church world today, the majority of God's sons and daughters are stuck on that far-off planet battling alien forces without the presence of God without being on the *Enterprise*. We need to fight through our present world and circumstances and be transported and taken into the Spirit to experience God's presence in a transforming life-changing way.

> We need to fight through our present world and circumstances and be transported and taken into the spirit to experience God's presence in a transforming lifechanging way.

In God's presence is the fullness of joy, and if you are not experiencing the fullness of joy, you are not experiencing the presence of God. The good news is, once you're beamed up into the *Enterprise*, it's the *Enterprise* that has the ability to deliver you from your problems and life-threatening situations, not you! You are now in a safe, strong place where clear communication takes place and assignments are given. An important truth to remember as you're stuck on that far-off planet is no matter how hard you try, there is no way of getting to the *Enterprise* in your own human effort. It must only be done by the work of Scotty, or in our case, the divine work of the Holy Spirit.

The Apostle Paul experienced being beamed up into God's presence. He writes, "I know a man in Christ who fourteen years ago was caught up to the third heaven. Whether it was in the body or out of the body, I do not know; God knows. And I know that this man whether in the body or apart from the body I do not know, but God knows—was caught up to paradise. He heard inexpressible things, things that man is not permitted to tell" (2 Corinthians 12:2–4, NIV). Paul had so many revelations and supernatural experiences that he was given a messenger from Satan to try to destroy him.

We need to start expecting and believing for supernatural experiences. The goal is not to have them so we can say, "Oh, that was wild," but every supernatural experience brings us closer to Jesus and reveals more of His nature. Also, it makes the work of evangelism and expanding the kingdom more effective.

> But every supernatural experience brings us closer to Jesus and reveals more of his nature.

God Says What?

God would say, "The world craves what you have available to you. They are seeking the supernatural. It's time you show them the right side of the supernatural and display My power so that the whole world may see My glory."

CHAPTER SIX

The Presence-Driven Life

Then Moses told the LORD, "If Your presence does not go with us, don't bring us up from here."
(Exodus 33:15, NIV)

Have you ever had a stubborn child who, even when he is told you are leaving, he just will not go? I have five children and had that experience many times. Moses was told to go into the land and settle into it. But he was stubborn in his attitude and said, "Not without Your presence." This attitude really pleased the Lord. We need to cultivate this kind of spiritual attitude within our lives, the attitude in which we simply tell the Lord that we need His presence, that we want His presence and desire Him more than anything, that without Him we do not want to do anything.

Presence People

The presence-driven life is the life that is driven and compelled to being transported into the presence of God. It releases the overflow of that experience into the world in the form of God encounters, such as signs, wonders and miracles. When Moses said, "I will not go without Your presence," he was, in fact, saying, "This will not be successful without God's presence." He was saying, "Without Your presence, Lord, how will we be successful and how will we be different?" To be presence-driven is to operate and live only from God's manifest presence. In other words, *every motive should lead us to His presence, and everything we attempt should be done from His presence.*

> He was saying, "Without your presence, Lord, how will we be successful and how will we be different?

We must realize without His presence and power, our enemy and the world will have the upper hand. Oh, sure, we might have some hand-held phasers that might only stun, but we need real power that will make a real difference. We cannot be satisfied in wounding and tolerating sin or any works of the enemy that God has already set us free from. We must be like Barney Fife on *The Andy Griffith Show* who often said, "Nip it in the bud!" Kill it and do not play around with things that will prevent you from the full benefit of God's presence.

Driving Options

In our journey on this earth, our lives can be driven by many things. In the story of Mary and Martha, we see that Martha was driven by things needed to be done, but Mary was driven by the presence of the Lord.

> As Jesus and His disciples were on their way, He came to a village where a woman named Martha opened her home to Him. She had a sister called Mary, who sat at the Lord's feet listening to what He said. But Martha was distracted by all the preparations that had to be made. She came to Him and asked, "Lord, don't You care that my sister has left me to do the work by myself? Tell her to help me!"
> "Martha, Martha," the Lord answered, "you are worried and upset about many things, but few things are needed—or indeed only one. Mary has chosen what is better, and it will not be taken away from her."
>
> (Luke 10:38–42, NIV)

Jesus replied, "Martha what are you doing?" Mary has chosen the one thing that is needed. One thing, and only one thing: to be in the presence of the Lord, and from that presence things will get done. It is really interesting why Jesus chose the word *needed* instead of another word. He said the one thing that was needful, Mary choose.

Men and women all over the world are driven and motivated by something or someone. A person can be goal-driven, and when he or she fulfills that goal, they set another one. These goals drive that person which is not a bad thing because goals help gauge success. Moses would say, "What good are goals when you're going into the Promised Land and facing giants with no presence?" Others are driven by their families. Everything they do is because of their family, and that keeps them driven to accomplish certain things. That is also not a bad thing because we should be motivated by our families and to take care of them.

Of course, there are many good things in the world that can drive a person, but *we can't sacrifice the best thing for the good things.* As Christians, we need to obey the principles of the Bible first and above all else. God says to seek first the kingdom, then everything else will be taken care of. In other words, whatever you do, remain in the manifest presence and seek daily instructions for your mission on earth and you will experience success. A person that is presence-driven is a person who is totally reliant on the presence of God. It's a person who does everything from the presence who makes things so much easier and more effective.

> There are many good things in the world that can drive a person, but *we can't sacrifice the best thing for the good things.*

What About Bob?

In the movie, *What About Bob?*, there is a scene with a very powerful spiritual truth that depicts the results of being presence-driven. The 1991 film is about a successful psychiatrist who loses his mind after one of his most dependent patients tracks him down during his family vacation. The great scene takes place when the doctor's daughter asked Bob if he wanted to go sailing. Bob immediately said, "No, no way," while he was visibly shaking. After a minute or so, Bob said, "I will try it. Yes, let's go sailing." The next scene you see is Bob tied to the front of the boat with a massive amount of ropes, yelling loudly, "I'm sailing! I'm sailing! Look, I'm sailing!" They finally come to shore, and he says these magical words, *"It was easy. I just let the boat do the work."* A presence-driven person is a person who is tied to the presence of God and lets the Holy Spirit do the work. A presence-driven life captures the presence of God and then follows His lead.

To be presence-driven is to wait on the Lord. It means to be transported into His presence and have encounters with the Lord in the secret place. Then we know what God wants when we leave. Jesus often withdrew from the crowds to encounter God. He also stated that He could do nothing without the Spirit. Jesus was God in the flesh, but put His divinity on hold and did everything as a man. *Life as a Christian is simple when you're tied to God's presence.* It's easy when you're aboard the *Enterprise* with all the weapons and shields all around to protect you. Life is very difficult when you're not tied to His presence and doing things in your weak, limited human strength.

> Life as a Christian is simple when you're tied to God's presence

That's because our work is a spiritual work and only the Spirit can accomplish that work. The Word of God tells us, "It is not by might nor by power, but by My Spirit." You would not take a bike and go sailing with it. Nor can you take the efforts of the flesh and accomplish spiritual things. Moses understood this truth, that he needed the presence of God.

Paralyzed Without the Presence

Moses was, in a sense, paralyzed without God's presence leading. Jesus lived His life in the same manner. Unfortunately, many Christians do not give the presence of God a second thought.

Moses was not going into the Promised Land without the presence of God. Moses was paralyzed in a purposeful way. He did not get ahead of God. He did not say, yes I know I have this communicator to the *Enterprise* and have access to it, but let me try this on my own. Moses would not even entertain any thoughts along those lines. Moses said to the Lord, "You have been telling me, 'Lead these people,' but You have not let me know whom You will send with me. You have said, 'I know you by name, and you have found favor with Me.' If You are pleased with me, teach me Your ways, so I may know You and continue to find favor with You. Remember that this nation is Your people." *The Lord replied, "My Presence will go with you, and I will give you rest."*

Then Moses said to Him, "If Your presence does not go with us, do not send us up from here. How will anyone know that You are pleased with me and with Your people unless You go with us? What else will distinguish me and Your people from all the other people on the face of the earth?" And the Lord said to Moses, "I will do the very thing you have asked, because I am pleased with you and I know you by name" (Exodus 33:12–17, NIV).

Moses was presence-driven. Notice again that God is everywhere, but He made a special point to tell Moses that His presence will go with him.

This was an emphasis on His manifest presence, not His general presence. Because Moses would not do anything without the presence of God, it pleased the Lord. We must live in the presence of the Lord. You may right now be driven and motivated by other things besides God's presence. You may feel burned out and frustrated. You may feel like you're defeated and saying to yourself, "What's the use?" We are at times driven by other things. Fear may drive you. You end up making bad decisions because of that. The past is the past. Begin the quest today for the difference maker.

The X-Factor

I have coached kids and noticed that what separates athletes from great athletes is what the sports world calls the X-factor. The X-factor is that something that no one can describe, but you know when it shows up. The X-factor that separates Christians from the world is the divine work of the presence of God. Without that, the church is no different from the world.

Have you ever heard someone say, if they were to convict you in a court of law for being a Christian, would they find any evidence to put you away? For some of us, they might find something and it might result in a small fine, no big deal. Others, by the works and the havoc they heaped upon the devil's kingdom, would probably get life in prison with no chance of parole. *What evidence in your life shows the world that you have just come from the presence of God?* How have you advanced the kingdom of God? In what ways have you destroyed the works of the devil? The world can imitate the things the church does very easily. These days, it is very hard to discern the difference at times between the church and the world. Moses clears this dilemma up in a very decisive way.

> What evidence in your life shows the world that you have just come from the presence of God?

Moses said to God, "What else will distinguish me and Your people from all the other people on the face of the earth?" Moses knew it was God's presence in Israel that set the people apart from all other nations. The same is true of the church of Jesus Christ today. The only thing that sets us apart from non-Christians is God's presence being manifested in our lives, leading us, guiding us and working His will in and through us.

Moses didn't care how other nations received their guidance, formed their strategies, ran their governments, or directed their armies. Moses was presence-driven. He believed there was only one thing he should strive for and only one thing he would react to, and that is the presence of God. We should operate on one principle alone. The only way for us to be guided or governed is to have the presence of God with us!

Think about this, if a church has the manifested presence of God in its midst, there won't be any hustle or bustle and there would not be a need for advertising. There will be no sweating or striving. The worship meetings won't be hurried along with three songs, an offering, and a short sermon. Instead, there will be a demonstration of the power and presence of God. Everyone who walks through the doors will sense it! *Ask yourself this—can your church still go on without God's presence?* Most of the churches today run on charismatic leaders and great orators. They hire great musicians and have great programs. *But they forget the one thing they need*—the manifested presence of God. All of those things are great and God has blessed us with those gifts, but the dangerous thing about that is *we become so enthralled with the blessings and gifts of God, that we forget God!*

Presence with a Punch

God's presence was so evident in Abraham's life, even the heathen around him recognized the difference between their lives and his. "Abimelech... spoke unto Abraham, saying, God is with thee in all that thou do" (Genesis 21:22, KJV). This heathen king was saying, Abraham, there's something different about you. God guides you, preserves you, and blesses you wherever you go! *That is the place we need to get to, where the presence of God is recognized by the world in our lives,* where the presence of God leaves people speechless and with no other option but to believe.

> *That is the place we need to get to, where the presence of God is recognized by the world in our lives.*

I remember when I was younger, my father had a similar thing happen to him. My father was a store owner, and one day, an employee came to him and asked how he has so much peace. The employee recognized that there was something different about my father. This man recognized the presence of the Lord. Not very much longer, that employee turned his life over to Christ and became a believer.

It is so vital that the presence of God's power works, and we get out of the way. Let's be like the neurotic patient Bob and just let the boat do the work. Let God's presence do the work; I do believe He would be much more qualified than you. I'm sure at times, just like me, that you get ahead of God and the end result is a total mess. Many times I have had to stop and repent and ask God's forgiveness for the mess I created because I untied the ropes and began paddling. How stupid was that when available to me was a sail forty feet high, catching a strong, mighty wind? *Sometimes, we are so far out of the zone that it's scary.*

David Was Presence-Driven

King David made God's presence a priority, so much so that God said of David that he was a man after God's own heart. David was radical when it came to seeking the presence of God. At one point, he was so excited about the return of the Ark that he was dancing in the streets, which made his wife very embarrassed. When he moved his capital to Jerusalem, he tried to bring the Ark of the Covenant to the city. The Ark was a box in the tabernacle. God's manifested presence was in the Ark, and David wanted God close.

> David arose and went with all the people who were with him to Baale-judah, to bring up from there the Ark of God which is called by the Name, the very name of the Lord of Hosts who is enthroned above the cherubim. (2 Samuel 6:2, ISV)

David realized that God's presence brought Israel victories against their enemies. Also, whenever the Ark was in Israel's possession, the nation would prosper. But King David went beyond the blessings of the Lord and right into His presence. *A lot of people seek the blessing of God but not really the presence of God,* not King David. All he was concerned about was God and being with Him.

> **A lot of people seek the blessing of God but not really the presence of God.**

> He said, "Whom have I in heaven, but You? And earth has nothing I desire besides You. My flesh and my heart may fail, but God is the strength of

my heart and my portion forever." (Psalm 73:25–26, NIV)

Is there anything in your life that you treasure more than the presence of God? There was none in the life of David. Of course, we do know what happened in David's life in regards to the sins he committed. However, after all that was said and done, it made him more determined to dwell in God's presence all the days of his life.

When we get to the place where nothing on earth matters more than the presence of God, then we will start living in the realm of God encounters. Everything of this world and every effort of the kingdom of darkness will try to stop you from encountering God. The enemies of God don't care if you pray, just don't experience God's presence. Sure, go to church, but don't encounter the Lord. Never activate that communicator and request to beam up into God's presence.

The prophet Isaiah told us to wait on the Lord. Jesus told His disciples to wait for the Holy Spirit. Jesus also was an example to us in waiting on God. Jesus said He never did anything unless He saw His Father doing it. Jesus always knew what God was saying and doing because He lived a presence-driven life. A.W. Simpson said about the apostles waiting in the Upper Room, "These waiting days were necessary to enable the disciples to realize their need, their nothingness, their failure and their dependence upon the Master. *They had to get emptied first before they would get filled."* (Emphasis mine) David knew his weakness; he expressed that in Psalm 51 when he said, "A broken and contrite heart the Lord will not despise." *David was a broken man, and that's why he desired God's presence in such a great way.*

> David was a broken man, and that's why he desired God's presence in such a great way.

God Says What?

God would say, "I know the battle and I know it's easy to get ahead of Me, but don't. You need My presence, and I want you to bask in it, and I want you to overflow in it, for it will make things in this world you do more effective and much easier. Wait as Mary did, and get alone with Me as Jesus did on a regular basis."

CHAPTER SEVEN

Faith That You Can Sleep On

And without faith it is impossible to please God, because anyone who comes to Him must believe that He exists and that He rewards those who earnestly seek Him.
(Hebrew 11:6, NIV)

If we want to enter into a building or home, or start a car, it takes a key or a set of numbers to a lock. Well, that is true also if we desire to enter or engage the spiritual world. We must have a key or a connector.

Faith is the key that connects the two worlds, the highway that brings together the physical and the spiritual. That's why the Word of God says that without faith it is impossible to please God. Those that come and pursue God must first believe that He is, and that He is a rewarder of those that strongly pursue Him. *For us even to enjoy His presence, we must believe that we can even experience it.* We must understand that God intends for this to happen and expects a dynamic, personal, real relationship with you. It's not for the afterlife when we get to heaven; Jesus came to make it happen now while we are on this earth.

> *For us even to enjoy his presence, we must believe that we can even experience it.*

We are in a church age right now where supernatural encounters with God are very rare. *A majority of people today have more experience with television than they do with God.* Many seasoned and experienced Christians have not seen a miracle nor have they experienced a supernatural event in their lifetime. That is because most of the church is not experiencing being transported into His presence. They are not experiencing God in a life-changing way. In Ezekiel 43:5, we read, "And the Spirit lifted me up and brought me into the inner court; and behold, the glory of the Lord filled the house." (NAS) Now that is an experience with the Lord. But most of us today have not experienced the Lord at all, and that, in turn, has resulted in very few God encounters that the world can witness.

Because of the lack of encounters experienced, the majority of the church do not really look for, or expect, such encounters. The saying is true: out of sight, out of mind. That is unfortunate and is also one of our enemies' number one targets. The enemy of God's church does not want His people getting familiar with moving in the supernatural and experiencing the presence and the power of God. He will deal with the little weapons of hand-held stunners, but not the photon torpedoes fired from the deck of the *Enterprise*. When that happens, he always loses. He can stand up against the works of our flesh, but anything done by the Spirit, forget it. He is finished. That's why there is a massive attack on the gifts of the Spirit. Everything will come against you to experience God, and live from His presence.

> That's why (there is a massive attack on the gifts of the Spirit) and that miracles are not for today.

Impossible to Please God Without Faith

Can you imagine promising your child that you will absolutely do something, only to hear them say, "I don't believe you, Dad," or "I don't believe you, Mom." That would be a very unpleasant thing to hear from one of your children that you love, that they have no faith in you or confidence in you. That is why it is impossible to please God our Father without faith. Without it, we are saying to Him, "I don't believe You, Father." *Lack of faith goes at the very heart and nature of God.* That is why there is so much written in the Scripture about the subject of faith. God has exalted His Word even above His name. That's why He really takes it personally when we act in unbelief.

> Lack of faith goes at the very heart and nature of God

Faith vs. Fear

I remember I was in the kitchen of a co-worker. His parents were in the house at that time. I knew this family were not Christians. I heard the Lord say I needed to talk with the father because he was having an affair, and the

Lord wanted to speak to him. I said, "Sure, Lord, not a problem. I will just go right up to him and say, 'Stop your affair now, thus says the Lord.'" I wish I had, but I became afraid and did nothing. In the following days, I wrestled with that, and two weeks later the wife found out, and they were eventually divorced. What happened to me was a God encounter that manifested in the form of a word of knowledge, one of the gifts of the Spirit. I since learned that *the gifts of the Spirit are not for us, but to bring other people into the kingdom of God.*

I could have decided to walk in faith and obeyed what the Lord told me. Who knows? That guy might have been really offended and could have gotten really angry. He could have thrown me out of the house at that moment. He could have also received the Word and repented. The point is, I should have acted and let all the possibilities fall where they may. Looking back, I knew the expectation of what God wanted. He wanted to restore that marriage and receive the glory for that God encounter. But I did not act on that expectation or on the word God gave me. So it takes courage and faith to move into the encounters of God. *When you are on the highway of faith to the presence of God, fear has no place.* In fact, if fear does arise, that means you have drifted off from the highway to His presence. Remember the words of Bob when he was tied to the boat. "That was easy. I just let the boat do the work." If it's a hard thing, you are the one doing the work, not the presence of God.

> *When you are on the highway of faith to the presence of God, fear has no place.*

I think of the story of David and Goliath. Everyone in the army of Israel was afraid. That is shocking in itself. Out of tens of thousands of men, there was not one man who would stand up to Goliath. But David did not even consider fear. He did not have one microscopic thought of fear. In fact, he did not even want the armor when going out to meet Goliath. Why did David not have any fear? Because he just came from the presence of the Lord. He was just aboard the *Enterprise* and was speaking with God directly. God's presence was overflowing

> *Why did David not have any fear? Because he just came from the presence of the Lord.*

out of him. Fear had no place to live. David was transformed and transported. David was about to experience the biggest God encounter of his life. When you're so filled up with the presence of God, and you have your rope tied to Him, fear has no room to stay. We all know what happened. David defeated the giant, and God received all the glory. One time I heard someone say, "Well if he had so much faith then why did he take five stones instead of one?" Another person responded, "The other four were for Goliath's brothers."

Faith You Can Sleep On

> Then He got into the boat and His disciples followed Him. Suddenly a furious storm came up on the lake, so that the waves swept over the boat. But Jesus was sleeping. The disciples went and woke Him, saying, "Lord, save us! We're going to drown!"
>
> He replied, "You of little faith, why are you so afraid?" Then He got up and rebuked the winds and the waves, and it was completely calm.
>
> The men were amazed and asked, "What kind of man is this? Even the winds and the waves obey Him!" (Matthew 8:27, NIV)

Jesus was at rest during the storm. David was at rest during his battle with Goliath. Peter, when he preached to the thousands, was at rest in his actions. Show me a person who is walking in faith, and I will show you a person who is at rest, no anxiety, no chaos and confident. This kind of faith and this kind of rest only comes from the presence of the Lord.

Imagine this, if you could travel in the future to the next day and observe an NFL football game and see the final score, then return again to the present time, you would have information that could get you a lot of money. Say you put your whole life savings on that game because you already knew the outcome. If your team was losing by twenty points, you still would be at peace and rest because you know what is going to take place. You are not moved by what the score is or what you see and observe. They don't sway you because you know! That's faith, my brother and sister. We know, therefore, we have rest and walk in peace not moved by any circumstances, but only by the Word of God. It's not the struggle of faith, but the rest of faith that brings results, faith that you can sleep on like Jesus in the boat.

People who pray for miracles usually don't get their miracles. It's the people who pray for courage to act on the Word of God and live in the realm of God who experience supernatural living and have God encounters. Once again, we who know God owe the world an encounter with God. Stepping out in faith takes courage. Stepping into a world that is anti-God, anti-miracles and anti-supernatural takes courage that is born from the presence of God. *However, the greater the battle, the greater the victory.* No matter where you are spiritually right now, you can begin to move more in the realm of God encounters. Start steering your spirit onto the highway of faith and into the presence of God, and watch what God's presence does through your life.

> *However, the greater the battle the greater the victory.*

God Says What?

I believe God would say, "I am pleased when My children believe in Me and act on My words. They are not moved by what they see or feel but only but what I say. I have stated in the Scriptures that when I return, will I find faith on the earth? Be a person of faith, and walk on My words as Peter walked on My words when I said get out of the boat and walk. Yes, he started to sink, but up to that point, he believed My words and acted on them. Keep your eyes on My words and believe them. I do not lie."

CHAPTER EIGHT

Magnetic Desire

As the deer thirsts for the streams of water, so I thirst for You, God.
Psalm 42:1

The deer feels himself almost entirely drained, with no strength left within him. He is nearly hunted down; the dogs are in full pursuit. He is dry, and he is drained with thirst. In a burning heat, he pants after the water. When he comes to the river, he plunges in with his last effort and escapes. Pursued, spent, and nearly ready to give up the ghost, the psalmist pants for God, for the living God, for He who can give life, and save from death.

Desire is the engine in our spiritual life and the attribute that God looks for when it comes to manifesting His presence. For example, Mary chose the one needed thing—that was to be in the presence of the Lord. David focused his desire on only one thing, and that was to dwell with God forever. Jesus referred to this as being hungry and thirsty for God's presence. Desire is vital to arriving in God's presence.

Magnetized Desire

Desire is the magnet that attracts the presence of God. I have a five-year-old granddaughter to whom I started to give tennis lessons. I love her, and if it were up to me, we would be training seven days a week. But the fact is, my presence in her life is dependent upon her and the desire she has to be with me. If her desire is strong, it will put a demand on my presence, and I will be there. The same it is with our Heavenly Father. He loves us and wants to fellowship with us continually. But our desire for Him is not attracting Him to us. Think about this: there are seven billion people in the world that have access to God. I believe He automatically responds and His presence is drawn by the magnetism of our desire. So desire is the

> *Desire is the magnet that attracts the presence of God*

engine, or the driving force, the navigational highway into the presence of God.

Not Dead Yet!

I have worked many years and in many hospitals as a respiratory therapist. One of my main jobs was to respond to code blues, which is when patients have cardiac arrests. Basically, the heart stopped, and we want to revive the patient, to bring him or her back to life physically. My job was to protect the airway and to resuscitate the patient by administering CPR. In these very intense moments, some were saved, and some did not make it. Spiritually speaking, many in the church need spiritual CPR. The Bible says that in the last days, so-called Christians will fall away from the truth and become cold in their relationship toward God and live as if they were dead spiritually. "Now the Spirit speaketh expressly, that in the latter times some shall depart from the faith, giving heed to seducing spirits, and doctrines of devils." (1 Timothy 4:1, KJV) Jesus asked the question whether He would find faith on the earth when He returns. I think it is very clear that the church of Jesus Christ needs a Holy Ghost revival. The church needs to be shaken out of her sleep. We need to cry out for a desire to go deeper into the presence of God.

This is the very beginning, the starting point to all spiritual encounters and the starting point to experiencing the presence of God. Without desire, God does not respond. The Word of God says, "Blessed are those who hunger and thirst after righteousness." For it's the hungry and the thirsty who shall be satisfied. The desire for God is even more important than God encounters themselves. *We should pursue His presence and seek His face and not His hands looking for more blessing* with an unequaled desire for Him and Him alone and nothing else.

Imagine being so thirsty that all you think about and all you care about is water. That's the type of desire that King David described. It's the strongest desire we have in the physical realm. That's the kind of desire that God our Father is longing for. Stop and think for a moment and meditate on the fact that *God's desire for us burns and He passionately wants you.* You might be saying, "I could never get to that level of desire." You can't because this is a divine work in our hearts that only the Spirit of God can bring us.

> God's desire for us burns and he passionately wants you.

But at the same time, we can get to that level of desire. It is possible to love the Lord with all our hearts, all our soul, all our might and strength. We need to get to the point where nothing else matters, and everything falls short to experiencing the presence of God. We say, "Just confess the Lord, and you are in!" He says, "Not everyone who says to me Lord, Lord will enter the kingdom." We say, "Just pray this prayer and it's done." He says, "If anyone would come after Me, he must deny himself, take up his cross and follow Me." We say, "Just come to the altar. It will only take a minute!" He says, "Make every effort to enter through the narrow door." Who do you think is right?

Spiritual CPR

I think it would be safe to say that at some point in our lives, we need spiritual CPR. We need to be spiritually awakened and revived to the things of God. Taking the acronym CPR, we can apply that to our spirits and start the reviving process. First, the "C" would be conviction—conviction of sin, conviction of not obeying God and the conviction of having no desire toward God. Now, conviction only comes from the Holy Spirit and cannot be manufactured. Conviction is different from condemnation. *Conviction is meant to move you toward God while commendation will move you away from God*, and condemnation is from the enemy. Conviction leads to repentance, and that's the first step into the presence of God. When talking about firing your desire, we must realize that this only comes from the work of the Spirit. In the book of Romans, it says, "Or do you despise the riches of His goodness, forbearance, and longsuffering, not knowing that the goodness of God leads you to repentance?" (Romans 2:4, NKJV)

The second letter is "P" for prayer. After being convicted and having repented, we must be diligent in strong prayer. I like the saying "pray hard." If you ever experienced a church service that just seemed dry and dead, that's because no work of the Holy Spirit is taking place. A person or a church is no greater than their prayer life. So when I am performing compressions on a body to try to revive it, it's like my prayers to God are pumping His life into our spirits and causing life to explode. In the book of James, it says that the effectual fervent prayer of a righteous man avails much. When we are performing chest compressions on someone, we are pumping hard. If we were not, no blood would be circulating, which means a person could also pray but not receive anything for many reasons.

The third letter is "R" for releasing. It's great to be revived and have prayer move God in us, but we must release what we have been given. We can't be like the Dead Sea in the Middle East, which is a sea with nothing living in it because it has no outflow. Rivers and streams flow into the sea, but it never releases into another body of water. Hence it is a dead sea. Way back in the old days, the Dead Sea was also called the stinky sea. That's what religion is like: stinky and dead. People stay away from religious people. Jesus had major problems with all the religious people of His time. Jesus did not like religion. So examine yourselves and ask if you need spiritual CPR and ask God to reveal to you the secret places of your heart. How am I advancing the kingdom of God? Am I releasing the power and the presence of God to the world around me? *Do I have a spiritual pulse or am I in need of some resuscitation?*

> *Do I have a spiritual pulse or am I in need of some resuscitation?*

How Bad Do You Want It?

You know from life experience that if a person really wants something they usually get it, no matter what the cost. In desperation, King David cried out, "Lord, hear my voice, let Thine ears be attentive to the voice of my supplications." (Psalm 103:2, KJV) This was a prayer of a desperate and dying man. David was just not uttering thought prayers. He was face down on the ground, broken and contrite, as he pleaded with God from the very depths of his heart. He was praying hard.

I remember a time of prayer our team had while on a mission trip to Belize. If you have ever taken a trip overseas, you have more than likely experienced more intense feelings of spiritual warfare. The supernatural and demonic activity is more prevalent in Third World countries. Don't be deceived, we have demonic activity here in our Western world also, but it manifests in different, less obvious ways. I heard someone say once that the demons over here are just more sophisticated.

The leader called the team together, and we had a time of corporate prayer. We prayed for about ten minutes. He stopped us and said, "Okay now let's really pray." Our prayers became more aggressive, more intense. Again, after about ten minutes he did the same as before. He said, "We have prayed, but now let's give it all we have." I can tell you that there was some spiritual damage done to the kingdom of darkness at that moment. That night, we had one of the most powerful services that I ever been in. Many God encounters took place in the form of physical healing, blind eyes being able to see, and it was amazing. We got to the point in prayer that we really wanted the presence of God to show up. More than that, we needed the presence of God to show up, or we were in trouble.

Enough of Dry-Eyed Desiring

Keith Green wrote an awesome song that portrays a desiring heart. The words are:

> My eyes are dry, My faith is old,
> My heart is hard, My prayers are cold,
> And I know how I ought to be,
> Alive to You, and dead to me.
> But what can be done,
> For an old heart like mine,
> Soften it up, With oil and wine,
> The oil is You, Your Spirit of love,
> Please wash me anew,
> With the wine of Your blood[2].

That is an awesome prayer, and it's the kind that touches the heart of God. David said almost the same thing when he wrote, "My sacrifice, O God, is a broken spirit; a broken and contrite heart You, God, will not despise." (Psalm 51:17, NIV). When we come to God with a genuine broken and desperate heart, He will not despise us or turn us away. We need to feel the zeal of the Lord. We need to be transported out of this earthly perspective and see things from God's perspective. We need to pray with passion and exhibit some holy anger and turn over some tables as Jesus did, spiritually speaking. (Don't go into your church next Sunday and flip over the coffee table). Our prayers and our desire for the things of God need to be fueled by the passion that the Lord has for a lost and dying world.

When we really do get transported, everything else become small. We see in the Spirit, and we sing and pray in the Spirit. We walk in the Spirit, and as naturally as a waterfall, we overflow with the presence and the power

---

2 Green, Keith. "My Eyes Are Dry", *No Compromise*. Sparrow Records SPD 1024, 1978.

of God.

God Does Not Play Games

God takes this issue very seriously. It's the simplest thing to be in the presence of God, and at the same time, it's the hardest thing for us. The Lord, for our own benefit, does not mess around with this issue. If it was easy, then all would enjoy His presence and flow in many God encounters. To be entrusted with God's presence, our hearts must be right. Like I mentioned before, we are right where we want to be in relation to desiring God. We need to have a Holy Spirit kicking to wake us up. Amos 6:1 says, "Woe to them that are at ease in Zion." (KJV). At that time, the people of Israel were very apathetic and lethargic concerning the things of God. This verse is a prophetic statement of the church today. We must realize that there is more for us and that God wants to do mighty things in us and through us. We need to repent and ask God to change our deceptive hearts. The fact is, right now the majority of the church is blind to their condition.

The persecuted churches around the world are really flourishing and expanding the kingdom. The Western church is so fat with materialistic things and has a we-can-do-it-by-ourselves mentality that we put ourselves in a position of not needing the presence of God. God shows up when our faith puts us in that position, that if He does not show up, we are in trouble.

Fast to Blast

Sometimes, we need an extra boost into the spiritual realm, and that's where fasting comes in. Sometimes, the transporter cannot lock in on us, and we have to adjust our position in order to be transported up to the *Enterprise*. If you really want to nuke your desire for God's presence and cause the highway of desire to take you to His presence, and you want to adjust your position to make it easier to get locked into, then implement a lifestyle of fasting. There is nothing magical about fasting, but what it does is help us focus on the Spirit and not the flesh. Fasting is like using a bazooka that blasts through the walls that may keep us from His presence.

We know that the disciples were sent out by Jesus to destroy the works of the devil. They were given authority and commissioned by Jesus. They were to heal and deliver people who were in bondage. We read in the book of Luke that they were having great success and they were happy and rejoicing over the power they were experiencing. But Jesus said to them "Nevertheless, do not rejoice that the spirits submit to you, but rejoice that your names are written in heaven." (Luke 10:20, NKJV) Jesus was telling them that there is a bigger picture. That the power of the kingdom is here, and you have access to it, not in the physical, but in the spiritual realm.

A little later, the disciples ran into a problem. They could not deliver one child who was tormented by a devil. Even though they had great success with all others, and were given that authority by Jesus, they could not cast out the demon in this child and make her free. After running to Jesus about the problem, Jesus replied, "This kind does not go out except by prayer and fasting." (Matthew 17:21, NKJV). They needed a greater weapon. That's what fasting does—it strengthens us in the spirit realm.

We read about an incident that Daniel experienced. He was praying for an answer and set himself on a fast until he received it. But the angel who was sent by God encountered some resistance, and it took him twenty-one days to get the answer to Daniel. Think about that. A powerful angel battled for twenty-one days to get the answer to Daniel. The invisible spiritual world is real, and it's high time the church starts exploring it. Imagine if Daniel just got frustrated and gave up his fast, he would not have received the answer. The bottom line is, the presence of God is a mighty weapon and fasting causes us in some way to have more of His presence and gives access to more of His power.

How Much Are You Willing to Pay

"If anyone comes to Me, and does not hate father and mother, wife and children, brothers and sisters—yes, even their own life—such a person cannot be my disciple." (Luke 14:26, NIV). These are powerful words that were said by Jesus. Of course, Jesus was not saying hate your family. But He was making a comparison that all other relationships in your life would seem like hate compared to your desire and love for God. *There is a cost to going deep into the presence of God and living a life of God encounters.* But there is also a cost for not experiencing the presence of God. That cost would be people not being introduced to God by you bringing them into a God encounter. Many people agree that it does

> There is a cost for going deep into the presence of God and living a life of God encounters.

cost us to be a radical follower of Christ. But many don't realize if they are not paying the cost to follow Jesus now, they will pay later. They will be sacrificing in other ways that are harmful to them and the world around them. There is always a cost for what we do or don't do, and it's always a choice that you have to make. A.W. Tozer, in *The Pursuit of God*, said,

> "Why do some persons 'find' God in a way that others do not? Why does God manifest His presence to some and let multitudes of others struggle along in the half-light of imperfect Christian experience? Of course, the will of God is the same for all. He has no favorites within His household. All He has ever done for any of His children, He will do for all of His children. The difference lies not with God but with us."

How desperate are you for His presence?

The Secret Place Only Holds One

The great man of God Leonard Ravenhill said, "Great eagles fly alone: Great lions hunt alone: Great souls walk alone, alone with God. Such loneliness is hard to endure and impossible to enjoy unless God accompanied. Prophets are lone men: they walk alone, pray alone, and God makes them alone." In our world today, it is difficult to find time alone. When we happen to find time alone, it is even more difficult to remain in a quiet attitude for periods of time and allow the presence of God to speak to us. But this is how God makes men and women. He does not have a cookie cutter factory and manufactures numerous robots, but He takes us one by one and molds us and transforms us into His image. "But Jesus often withdrew to lonely places and prayed" (Luke 5:16, NIV). Why did Jesus withdraw often? Why did He look for lonely places? This is where we meet God, and this is where He overflowed with His presence. God desires above everything else an intimate relationship with us. These lonely places were the strength

> Great eagles fly alone: Great lions hunt alone: Great souls walk alone, alone with God

of Jesus. When He went into the desert to be tempted by the devil, He was led by the Spirit. When He departed the lonely desert place, He was full of the Spirit and full of power.

God Says What?

I believe God would say, "You can have a desire that is on fire. He would say, I want to do the work in you, and I want to fellowship with you in a deep and intimate way. That's My desire for you and is totally explosive with passion for you. I love you unconditionally, and I see in you only potential to do great things in My kingdom. He would say, Stretch yourself and hunger and thirst for Me so that I can take you to higher levels in the kingdom."

> But this is how God makes men and women. He does not have a cookie cutter factory and manufactures numerous robots, but he take us one by one and molds us and transforms us into his image

CHAPTER NINE

Revelation Revolution

*Where there is no revelation, people cast off restraint;
but blessed is the one who heeds wisdom's instruction.*
(Proverbs 29:18, NIV)

This verse is referring to vision and revelation. Back then, the people received the word of the Lord from prophets and seers. The lack of the Word of God—that is, the revelatory word from God—causes confusion and bad decisions. Today, we have the Holy Spirit within us that opens and reveals God's written word. We need the revelation of God daily, for man shall not live by bread alone but by every word (*rhema* is the word for revelation) of God.

As was stated before, revelation causes us to navigate into deeper experience with God's presence. Once our desire and faith bring us into the presence of God, then the highway of revelation is never-ending. There are things God desires to reveal to us, but it is not all at once. Jesus, instructing His disciples to pray the Lord's Prayer said this, "Give us today our daily bread." That, my brother and sister, is daily manna, daily words from the Lord. As Jesus said to Peter, "Blessed are you, Peter, for flesh and blood had not revealed this to you but My Father in heaven" *Our daily bread is revelation from the Holy Spirit.*

> *Our daily bread is revelation from the Holy Spirit.*

The Power of Revelation

The story of the great revivalist John Wesley shows us the power of a single revelation. John Wesley was a great theologian, but early in his life, he struggled. Wesley faithfully served as a priest in England and the United States. He committed himself to Bible study, prayer and fasting, and serving others. He acknowledged that Jesus is the Son of God, but he studied only with the mind. He didn't understand in his heart that the promises of God were true for his every need. Then at the age of thirty-five, he was transformed. During a meeting with fellow Christians at Aldersgate Street in London, Wesley had a deeply personal encounter with God. While Martin Luther's preface to the commentary on the book of Romans was being read, Wesley became electrified. He called the experience a "quickening" in his soul. He said his heart was strangely warmed, much like the two men on the road to Emmaus when they said, "Did our hearts not burn within us" while they received revelation. No longer were his beliefs merely intellectual, but he now had revelation and his eyes were opened. We know that from that point on, he changed the world. Wesley went from being a dead theologian to a powerful living Christian. Revelation gives life and energizes our relationship with God.

Over and over throughout the Scripture, God has referred to people that have eyes yet don't see. Also, He says that they have ears but don't hear, and minds yet don't understand. Most of these remarks are directed to religious people and not the world. Unless we can get beyond this physical world and see into the spiritual world and hear from God, then we will go no further into the presence of God. In Ephesians 3:19, Paul talks about a love that surpasses knowledge. He is saying there is knowledge, and then there is knowledge at a different level, a different realm.

Revelation takes us into God's presence, but it also takes us deeper into His presence once we enter into it. It is crucial that we experience God ourselves, because it's from those experiences that we receive revelation, and it is revelation that will propel us into God encounters. Considering which comes first, receiving revelation or being in God's presence is a little like the chicken and the egg. We need revelation in regards to entering into God's presence, but on the other hand, we only get revelation from God Himself.

Revelation is something that cannot be learned or read about, but only something that can be given. Going to church will not necessarily bring an experience with God. In fact, just because you are extremely blessed by God does not mean you are experiencing God. The Bible says that God rains down blessing on the just and unjust. Your blessing does not mean you're amazing, it just means that God is amazing. You must encounter God yourself. Revelation is not taught, revelation is only caught by

> God has no grandchildren he has only sons and daughters.

being in the presence of God. Once again, God has no grandchildren he has only sons and daughters. To be honest with you, it sort of concerns me in even writing this book. I think the body of Christ is saturated with so much knowledge, but very little revelation. Our verse for this chapter is Proverbs 29:18 which says that people without revelation have no direction. You can be a person who knows everything there is to know about the Bible. You can quote a thousand Bible verses but still not have revelation on what you are reading. Revelation only comes from the impartation of the Holy Spirit. Again, in the book of Matthew, we read:

> When Jesus came to the region of Caesarea Philippi, He asked His disciples, "Who do people say the Son of Man is?" They replied, "Some say John the Baptist; others say Elijah; and still others, Jeremiah or one of the prophets.""But what about you?" He asked. "Who do you say I am?" Simon Peter answered, "You are the Messiah, the Son of the living God." Jesus replied, "Blessed are you, Simon son of Jonah, for this was not revealed to you by flesh and blood, but by My Father in heaven. (Matthew 16:13-18, NIV)

Peter had special knowledge that no one else had. That knowledge was given by God alone, and that is revelation. It's revelation that will take you deeper into the paths of God's presence. The Bible teaches, "The beginning of wisdom is this: Get wisdom, and whatever you get, get insight." In all your gathering and all your getting above everything else, get revelation. Have you ever heard the saying, you don't know what you don't know. Well, we do not know until the Holy Spirit reveals it to us. I am sure this has happened to you—you read a passage of Scripture a hundred times, and you think you know it, but then you read it again and bam! You now have a new meaning of it that changes your life. That is revealed knowledge.

Revelation means the communication of knowledge to man by a divine or supernatural agency. That is what happened to Peter when answering Jesus's question about who He was. The Word of God, or the Bible, is truth and it is knowledge concerning the things of God. But that word needs to become revealed to us by the Holy Spirit. Ask yourself why doesn't everyone see that Christ died for them? It says that right in the Bible. That's because those who do not believe have not had a revelation of that truth. Once we get revelation, we tie that to the presence of God, and once we are in His presence, we receive more revelation and we go even deeper into God's presence.

Apostle Paul's Prayer

This is one of the most important prayers that Paul prayed for the body of Christ. In Ephesians 1:17-18, he says,

> I keep asking that the God of our Lord Jesus Christ, the glorious Father, may give you the Spirit of wisdom and revelation so that you may know Him better. I pray that the eyes of your heart may be enlightened in order that you may know the hope to which He has called you, the riches of His glorious inheritance in His holy people, and His incomparably great power for us who believe. That power is the same as His mighty strength. (NIV)

He says I want you to have revelation so that you will know Him. Without revelation, you really do not know the Lord. Satan has blinded the minds of the world, or they would see the glorious gospel of Christ. The world needs a revelation that Christ died for them. Through releasing God encounters and the presence of God in this world, revelation will come to them, and repentance will take place. The spirit of wisdom is what Paul is praying we receive.

Wisdom in Greek is *sophias*, which means insight or wisdom not naturally attained. The word revelation in this verse in Greek is *apokeluposis*, which means something veiled or hidden then suddenly appears or becomes visible. You could translate this verse like this, "I keep asking that God, our Lord Jesus may give you special insight. I am talking about wisdom that is not naturally attained." This is the divine moment when the curtains are drawn back, and you are supernaturally enabled to see what you could not see by yourself. This is what Jesus was referring to when Peter said, "He is the Christ the Son of the living God." Jesus said this knowledge did not come from man. Paul's thorn in the flesh was due to his many revelations and supernatural experiences because of these surpassingly great revelations.

"Therefore, in order to keep me from becoming conceited, I was given a thorn in my flesh, a messenger of Satan, to torment me" (2 Corinthians 12:7, NIV). Paul not only prayed that we would have revelations, but he also had them, and they were normal in his life.

The Spirit Realm Revealed

The kingdom of God and the kingdom of darkness are in a great battle, and we are smack dab right in the middle. Each is influencing us and speaking to us. We have to decide which one to listen to. In the book of 2 Kings, there is a story that gives us an example of the two worlds and how God is needed for us to see and hear from His kingdom. We need revelation to navigate into the spiritual realm and into God's presence.

> Now the king of Aram was at war with Israel. After conferring with his officers, he said, "I will set up my camp in such and such a place." The man of God sent word to the king of Israel: "Beware of passing that place, because the Arameans are going down there." So the king of Israel checked on the place indicated by the man of God. Time and again Elisha warned the king, so that he was on his guard in such places. This enraged the king of Aram. He summoned his officers and demanded of them, "Tell me! Which of us is on the side of the king of Israel?" "None of us, my lord the king," said one of his officers, "but Elisha, the prophet who is in Israel, tells the king of Israel the very words you speak in your bedroom." "Go, find out where he is," the king ordered, "so I can send men and capture him." The report came back: "He is in Dothan." Then he sent horses and chariots and a strong force there. They went by night and surrounded the city. When the servant of the man of God got up and went out early the next morning, an army with horses and chariots had surrounded the city. "Oh no, my lord! What shall we do?" the servant asked. "Don't be afraid," the prophet answered. "Those who are with us are

more than those who are with them." And Elisha prayed, "Open his eyes, Lord, so that he may see." Then the Lord opened the servant's eyes, and he looked and saw the hills full of horses and chariots of fire all around Elisha. As the enemy came down toward him, Elisha prayed to the Lord, "Strike this army with blindness." So he struck them with blindness, as Elisha had asked. (2 Kings 6, NIV)

We must have our eyes and ears opened to the spiritual kingdom, or we will never encounter God the way that He wants us to. Paul also said, I do not look at what is seen, but I look to what is unseen. Jesus, speaking about the religious leaders of His day, said they have eyes but see not, and they have ears but are deaf. We have to get to the place where we see what God is saying. I will repeat that again—we must see what God is saying, and not only hear. Many Christians can quote Scripture, but not understand its meaning.

Revelation is like a light bulb that comes on, and the only one who can flick the switch is the Holy Spirit. You only acquire more revelation as you walk in and obey the revelation you have now. I have a Muslim friend who is aware of the verse that says Jesus is the only way to heaven. In fact, he can quote it, and he can elaborate on it the correct way. But he has no revelation on it and it really means nothing to him. That's why we need revelation. The Word of God declares with all your getting, make sure you get revelation.

The Rhema and the Logos

The Greek word for the written word (the Bible) is *logos*. The Greek word for the spoken word (revelation) is *rhema*. When Jesus said that man shall not live by bread alone, but by every Word of God, the word translated there is the word *rhema*—God's spoken word or revelation. Our Father wants to speak to us and wants to reveal Himself to us. Well, you might say, all I need is my Bible. If that was the case, why did the Holy Spirit come to be our helper and strength? The written word needs to become revealed in our hearts.

The disciples experienced this after Jesus's resurrection.

On the first day of the week, very early in the morning, the women took the spices they had prepared and went to the tomb. They found the stone rolled away from the tomb, but when they entered, they did not find the body of the Lord Jesus. While they were wondering about this, suddenly two men in clothes that gleamed like lightning stood beside them. In their fright, the women bowed down with their faces to the ground, but the men said to them, "Why do you look for the living among the dead? He is not here; He has risen! Remember how He told you, while He was still with you in Galilee: 'The Son of Man must be delivered over to the hands of sinners, be crucified, and on the third day be raised again.'" Then they remembered His words.

When they came back from the tomb, they told all these things to the Eleven and to all the others. It was Mary Magdalene, Joanna, Mary the mother of James, and the others with them who told this to the apostles. But they did not believe the women, because their words seemed to them like nonsense. Peter, however, got up and ran to the tomb. Bending over, he saw the strips of linen lying by themselves, and he went away, wondering to himself what had happened.

Now that same day two of them were going to a village called Emmaus, about seven miles from Jerusalem. They were talking with each other about everything that had happened. As they talked and discussed these things with each other, Jesus Himself came up and walked along with them; but they were kept from recognizing Him. He asked them, "What are you discussing together as you walk along?" They stood still, their faces downcast. One of them, named Cleopas, asked Him, "Are you the only one visiting Jerusalem who does not know the things that have happened there in these days?"

"What things?" He asked. "About Jesus of Nazareth," they replied. "He was a prophet, powerful in word and deed before God and all the people. The chief priests and our rulers handed Him over to be sentenced to death, and they crucified Him; but we had hoped that He was the one who was going to redeem Israel. And what is more, it is the third day since all this took place. In addition, some of our women amazed us. They went to the tomb early this morning but didn't find His body. They came and told us that they had seen a vision of angels, who said He was alive. Then some of our companions went to the tomb and found it just as the women had said, but they did not see Jesus. He said to them, "How foolish you are, and how slow to believe all that the prophets have spoken! Did not the Messiah have to suffer these things and then enter His glory?" And beginning with Moses and all the Prophets, He explained to them what was said in all the Scriptures concerning Himself.

As they approached the village to which they were going, Jesus continued on as if He were going farther. But they urged Him strongly, "Stay with us, for it is nearly evening; the day is almost over." So He went in to stay with them. When He was at the table with them, He took bread, gave thanks, broke it and began to give it to them. Then their eyes were opened and they recognized Him, and He disappeared from their sight. They asked each other, "Were not our hearts burning within us while He talked with us on the road and opened the Scriptures to us?" (Luke 24:1-32, NIV)

They did not even recognize Jesus. Their eyes had to be opened to see the truth. It is the same for us in reading the Scriptures. Our eyes have to be opened, and we need revelation to come. What has revelation got to do with being transported into God's presence? Revelation energizes faith, it motivates our spirits with passion and hunger. It takes the things that are mundane and lifeless and breathes life into them. Unless you have revelation of being in the presence of God, you will not see it or believe it. Oh, you might acknowledge it as a fact, but that's about it. God's revelation to you of being translated into His presence will not only cause you to strive for that, but it will give you faith for it.

> Revelation energizes faith, it motives our spirits with passion and hunger and takes the things that are but mundane and lifeless and breaths life into them.

God Says What?

I believe God would say, "I so much want to reveal Myself to you in ways that you cannot even imagine. I want to open up the spirit realm to you and draw you into it so that you may partake of heaven and My kingdom while you live on this earth. Press in and do not settle for what is good and miss out on what is excellent and available to you."

CHAPTER TEN

Weapons of Mass Destruction

The weapons we fight with are not the weapons of
the world. On the contrary, they have divine power to
demolish strongholds.
(2 Corinthians 10:4, NIV)

Many believers do not want to acknowledge that we are in a war, a spiritual battle for the souls of men. That's why the Apostle Paul talks so much about this subject of warfare. He encourages us to be a good soldier and to stay sober. Mature Christians know we enter God's presence because of our love for Him and His love for us. However, make no mistake about it. God wants us to leave His presence prepared and equipped to do battle.

Find a Phone Booth

"It's a bird! No, it's a plane! No! It's Superman!" I'm sure everyone has heard those lines in Superman cartoons or in the movies. Superman is a very popular fiction action superhero. A closer look into the make-believe character of Superman reveals spiritual truths that apply to the world in which we live. Clark Kent, the scared, timid, and clumsy nerd is the other half of the story. But when Clark Kent goes into a phone booth . . . Bam! Watch out! He becomes Superman.

We see this same story taking place in the Scripture with the Apostle Peter. A weak coward is transformed into a superman. At one point, just before Jesus was going to be crucified, we see Peter afraid, timid and shaking because a teenage girl recognized him, and said that he was with Jesus. At that point, Peter replied that she is crazy, denied knowing Jesus, and ran off. Not long after this incident, Peter, after entering the Upper Room in prayer, exited that room, not a scared little rabbit, but a superman. He became a super spiritual giant and preached the most famous sermon ever. Well, what made the difference in Peter? How can somebody make a complete turnaround? How can someone who could not even admit to a teenage girl he was with Jesus become someone who changed a whole city for Christ? Peter had no phone booth to enter into and be transformed, but he did have a room where he met the presence of God and became completely transformed.

The Hidden Army of Giants

Today there is hidden an army of supermen and superwomen, waiting to be released into this world, as was Peter on the day of the Pentecost. There are many in the kingdom of God doing battle on the frontlines, not for a glory-seeking motive but out of humility with advancing the kingdom of God as their motive. They are all warriors for God and deadly in the spiritual realm.

> Many today in the church don't know they are superhuman, they don't realize that there is such a person in them or they do give it any thought.

Many today in the church don't know they are superhuman. They don't realize that there is such a person in them or they don't give it any thought. But they are out there in the world, millions upon millions and soon they will have their eyes opened. Just like Peter and the other 120 who entered the Upper Room and were transformed into spiritual giants and operating from a power of a different world, the church will wake up and start recognizing that they, too, are from another world and another kingdom. Instead of entering the nearest phone booth, we, who are the church, will enter into the Holy of Holies, the secret place of the Most High, to be transformed and be transported into His presence, that place where God meets with us alone.

Like Moses who met God in the desert, and Joseph who met God in captivity, and like the three Hebrew children who had an encounter with God in the fire, so we can encounter God, and He will meet us and transform us. Today, because of what Jesus did for us on the cross, we can enter into the throne room of God. We enter in boldly knowing that we can be transformed by His presence into spiritual supermen and superwomen who have power over this earthly kingdom. Did you ever stop and consider why Jesus cursed the fig tree when he found no fruit on it, and the next morning the disciples found the tree dead? It was to show the disciples that if they had faith nothing was impossible, even power over the natural realm.

The church of our Lord Jesus is infused with, and has available, the most powerful weapon in existence. But, at the same time, the church is displaying very little of that power. *You would think that after existing for more than two thousand years, we would be a little further in our efforts in evangelism and in expanding the rule and kingdom of God.* It does not take a genius or somebody with great spiritual discernment to figure out that something is wrong.

> *You would think that after existing for more than two thousand years, we would be a little further in our efforts in evangelism and in expanding the rule and kingdom of God.*

God's Favorite and Most-Used Phrase

Have you ever noticed in reading the Scripture that God has always emphasized to His leaders that He will be with them? Or His presence will go with you? Why did He not say, "I will give you other means to be victorious?" God's victory for us and for all the battles that faced Israel and its leaders have always been tied to His presence. God's presence is in itself the most powerful weapon in existence.

> "Let God arise, let His enemies be scattered: let them also that hate Him flee before Him. As smoke is driven away, so drive them away: as wax melteth before the fire, so let the wicked perish at the presence of God. But let the righteous be glad; let them rejoice before God: yea, let them exceedingly rejoice." (Psalm 68:1-3, KJV)

Also in Psalms, we read, "I will praise thee, O Lord, with my whole heart; I will shew forth all Thy marvelous works. I will be glad and rejoice in Thee: I will sing praise to Thy name, O thou Most High. When mine enemies are turned back, they shall fall and perish at Thy presence." (Psalm 9:1-3, KJV)

Here's the amazing part: we have access to His presence. He not only dwells within us, but also comes upon us, and reveals His presence. Actually, the Bible teaches us that we also have an arsenal of weapons. Here are just a few of the weapons God has given us. These weapons are not only to be used to live a victorious life, but also to bring us closer to God and His presence and have a strong, intimate relationship with him.

The Weapon of the Word of God

"For the Word of God is alive and active. Sharper than any double-edged sword, it penetrates even to dividing soul and spirit, joints and marrow; it judges the thoughts and attitudes of the heart" (Hebrew 4:12, NIV). Talk about a weapon of mass destruction.

Jesus used this weapon when He was tempted by the devil in the desert. Jesus answered, "It is written: 'Man shall not live on bread alone, but on every word that comes from the mouth of God'"(Matthew 4:4, NIV). When you speak God's word into a situation, God's presence and power are released if spoken in faith. In Ephesians, it states, "Take the helmet of salvation and the sword of the Spirit, which is the Word of God." When you speak God's word, you begin to activate God encounters, because God's word does not return to Him empty, but it accomplishes that which it is sent to do.

Now, when we receive revelation of His Word, that's when it becomes explosive, and that revelation comes from being on the bridge of the *Enterprise* or in the presence of God. The Romans used a short double-edged sword called a *gladius*. Because it was smaller and lighter, it was easier for a soldier to carry for a long distance and easier to handle and maneuver in a battle. While a shield, a helmet, and breastplate were used only for defense purposes, a sword was used for offense as well as defense. For defense, a soldier wielded the sword to deflect the enemy's blows. As an offensive weapon, the sword was used to attack an enemy until he was seriously wounded or killed.

The word can pull down the strongholds of Satan like a missile. Through this weapon, not only can we resist the devil's influence in our own lives, but also we can destroy his influence in the lives of others. "For the weapons of our warfare are not carnal, but mighty in God for pulling down strongholds and casting down arguments and every high thing that exalts itself against the knowledge of God, bringing every thought into captivity to the obedience of Christ" (2 Corinthians 10:4-5, NAS). Again, Jesus used the word to defeat the devil's attacks.

The Weapon of Prayer

> For verily I say unto you, That whosoever shall say unto this mountain, Be thou removed, and be thou cast into the sea; and shall not doubt in his heart, but shall believe that those things which he says shall come to pass; he shall have whatsoever he says. Therefore I say unto you, What things so ever ye desire, when ye pray, believe that ye receive them, and ye shall have them. (Mark 11:22–24, KJV).

We underestimate the power of prayer. Sometimes, we use it as a last resort when it should be the first thing we go to. The body of Christ is so disillusioned with unanswered prayers, that when we do pray, it's like a fifty-fifty chance. The power of prayer is based on how we believe, for the Bible says the prayer of faith is powerful and effective. Faith is confidence in the ability of God, and that only comes from knowing God in a personal way. The Bible says the effectual, fervent prayer will do much. So if there are prayers that do much, then that would leave us also with prayers that do little. The key is that we need to *say* unto the mountain and not *pray* unto the mountain. This kind of praying again only comes from being transformed in the presence of God.

The Weapon of Worship

By placing ourselves before Him in a place of adoration or a place of worship, we make room for Him; and through focusing our attention on Him, we increase our awareness of His presence. Learning how to soak in God's presence through worship is one of the most valuable things we can do with our time. In James 4:8, we read God has promised that as we draw near to Him, He will draw near to us and we will experience Him with us in ever-increasing measures. This is one way of abiding in the presence of God, by abiding in worship.

"As they began to sing and to praise, the Lord set ambushes against the men of Ammon and Moab and Mount Seir who were invading Judah, and they were defeated" (2 Chronicles 20:22, NIV). We know from the Scripture that God inhabits the praises of His people. There is nothing like changing the whole atmosphere when you begin to praise and worship the Lord. There are so many weapons that we have available to us, but the most important thing to remember is that they all operate from the presence of the Lord in our lives. God's presence is connected to all these weapons, and God expects us to use them. Why else did He give us all the weapons? Certainly not to play GI Joe.

> *Learning how to soak in God's presence through worship is one of the most valuable things we can do with our time.*

Can the Presence of God Be Detected in Your Life?

"When they saw the courage of Peter and John and realized that they were unschooled, ordinary men, they were astonished and they took note that these men had been with Jesus. And seeing the man who had been healed standing there with them, they had nothing to say in response." (Acts 4:12-13, NIV)

This is what the crowd noticed about the apostles Peter and John when they had been with Jesus. Also, they could not dispute the miracles that they were doing and the healed man who was standing right by them. Evangelism is made very easy when we overflow with the presence of God in our lives. It's hard when we don't have His presence, and very little happens because of that absence.

The early church and the apostles were walking so much in the supernatural that the crowds just wanted to get close to them, hoping that even their shadow might fall on them so that the sick could be healed. That is amazing, but we know shadows don't heal people and that only the presence of God does. That's what was happening in the early church. Can you imagine walking down the street and you hear someone say to you, "What's up with you? I feel and sense something different about you. Oh, and another thing, when you walked by, the pain from my cancer was gone." That would be awesome and a great testimony for God. You're probably saying,

> *But we know shadows don't heal people and that only the presence of God does.*

"Yes, that would be great, but that would never happen." Well, all I can say is what God says in His Word, be it according to how you believe. It is possible; all things are possible to those who believe.

The Power of His Presence Displayed

In John chapter 18, Jesus said something that caused the Roman soldiers who came to arrest Him to fall down. As soon as He said unto them, "I am He," they went backwards, recoiled and fell to the ground, struck down by a power such as that which smote Saul of Tarsus and his companions to the earth. It was the glorious effulgence of the majesty of Christ that overpowered them. "This, occurring before His surrender, would show His power over His enemies, and so the freedom with which He gave Himself up" (Meyer commentary). In Acts, Paul writes, "We all fell to the ground, and I heard a voice saying to me in Aramaic, 'Saul, Saul, why do you persecute Me? It is hard for you to kick against the goads'" (Acts 26: 14, NIV). Again, it was the presence of the Lord that caused him to fall to the ground—just from His voice and presence.

I recall a service that at one point, the minister shared that the presence of the Holy Spirit was really strong and moving in the audience. Right at that time, about half the church fell back into their seats in a powerful way, and I was one of them. All I recall was looking up at my wife and asking what happened. It was the power of His presence.

God's presence was so evident in Abraham's life, even the heathen around him recognized the difference between their lives and his. "Abimelech said unto Abraham, saying, God is with thee in all that you do" (Genesis 21:22, KJV). This heathen king was saying, "There is something different about you." As we would say today, "You have the X-factor with you, something that makes you special and different." We know that to be the presence of God.

God also promised Joshua that no enemy that he came against could stand against him when God's presence was with him. "There shall not any man be able to stand before thee all the days of thy life: as I was with Moses, so I will be with thee: I will not fail thee, nor forsake thee. Be strong and of good courage" (Joshua 1:5–6, KJV). Again, it's the presence of God that makes Joshua successful and mighty. We need to use the presence of God as a mighty weapon in our lives. He wants us to; that's what He made available to us on the day of Pentecost.

One of my favorite stories is the story of Gideon. The Lord came down to Gideon and said, "the Lord is with you, mighty warrior. Go in your might and save Israel." When the Lord said "your might" He was referring to His presence in the previous verses. God was saying that Gideon's might was His presence. His presence is the mighty weapon that we need in our lives.

King David Knew the Power of His Presence

> If it seems good to you and if it is the will of the Lord our God, let us send word far and wide to the rest of our brothers throughout the territories of Israel, and also to the priests and Levites who are with them in their towns and pasturelands, to come and join us. Let us bring the Ark of our God back to us, for we did not inquire of it during the reign of Saul. (1 Chronicles 13:2b–3, NIV).

David wanted the presence of the Lord back in Israel. King Saul lost the Ark to the Philistines in battle. Under Saul, worship of the Lord had suffered and was not a priority. Saul had disobeyed the Lord's direction through Samuel (1 Samuel 13:13; 15:11). The Ark had been lost a generation before and never returned to its place in the tabernacle (1 Samuel 4–6). In his fear and jealousy, Saul had slaughtered the priests who tended the tabernacle at Nob (1 Samuel 22:18–19). He was no longer able to seek the Lord because Abiathar, the remaining priest, had taken the ephod with him when he had fled to David (1 Samuel 22:20, 23:6). The worship of God was so damaged and forgotten, Saul was reduced to seeking guidance from the witch of Endor, a spiritualist medium (1 Samuel 28). But David realized the importance of the presence of God. David had the testimony of the Lord about being a man after God's own heart. I believe it was because of his love for God's presence and how he treated His presence. David knew when they had the Lord's presence or the Ark in their midst and treated His presence in a right way, they were victorious over their enemies. It's the same today and in our lives. If we treat the presence of God right and grieve not His Holy Spirit, then we will walk in victory over our flesh and the devil.

Guard the Presence of the Lord

The presence of the Lord must not be taken lightly. Just ask Ananias and his wife.

> Now a man named Ananias, together with his wife Sapphira, also sold a piece of property. With his wife's full knowledge, he kept back part of the money for himself, but brought the rest and put it at the apostles' feet. Then Peter said, Ananias, how is it that Satan has so filled your heart that you have lied to the Holy Spirit and have kept for yourself some of the money you received for the land? Didn't it belong to you before it was sold? And after it was sold, wasn't the money at your disposal? What made you think of doing such a thing? You have not lied just to human beings but to God. When Ananias heard this, he fell down and died. And great fear seized all who heard what had happened. Then some young men came forward, wrapped up his body, carried him out, and buried him. About three hours later, his wife came in, not knowing what had happened. Peter asked her, "Tell me, is this the price you and Ananias got for the land?" "Yes," she said, "that is the price." Peter said to her, "How could you conspire to test the Spirit of the Lord? Listen! The feet of the men who buried your husband are at the door, and they will carry you out also." At that moment, she fell down at his feet and died. Then, the young men came in and, finding her dead, carried her out and buried her beside her husband. Great fear seized the whole church and all who heard about these events." (Acts 5:1-10, NIV)

The presence of the Lord was offended and lied to, and judgment came to these two.

Another incident about mishandling the Lord's presence was when King David was transporting the Ark which contained the presence of the Lord. Another man died because he did not handle the Lord's presence in the right way. The Word of God strictly warns us, "Do not grieve the Holy Spirit of God, with whom you were sealed for the day of redemption." (Ephesians 4:30, NIV) Really, we need a good healthy dose of the fear of God back into the church today.

God Says What?

I believe God would say, "Wrap yourself in My presence and delight yourself in the Lord. I do want you to experience joy to the fullest, and it is only found as you dwell in My presence. My son, King David, sought My presence with his whole heart and he only had one desire—that was to dwell in My presence. He was a man after My own heart."

CHAPTER ELEVEN

The Island of Misfits

But God chose the foolish things of the world to shame the wise; God chose the weak things of the world to shame the strong.
(1 Corinthians 1:27, NIV)

What's Crazy?

I don't think there is such a thing as crazy in this world any longer. Let me explain. The world is so crazy that if you do act crazy, it's normal. People who believe in the supernatural and living heaven on earth sometimes have a stigma. I don't think so!

My wife and I were watching a TV program about strange addictions people have. They showed a woman who was addicted to cat food. They showed another woman addicted to drinking paint. Another woman acted like a pony and bought horse stuff for herself. They showed a guy who was literally in love with his car. It was hard to watch. I turned to my wife and said, "Do not call me crazy anymore." After watching that, she agreed.

The Lord brought this thought to me and said, "Joe, what is crazy? Is believing that I want to work supernaturally through you or not working through you? Is it crazy living a successful Christian life in your natural flesh and strength or relying upon My presence, My power and gifts of the Spirit? It is not crazy to think on heavenly things? To think on miracles and signs and wonders? To have the mind of Christ and to think the way He would think?"

In fact, we are told to do so. It's not crazy to believe in being transported or translated or transformed in and by the Spirit and to have miracles being released from our lives. Being a Christian, being born from above by the Spirit, and having the Holy Spirit dwell in us, it would be crazy to believe that nothing like that can or will be done in this lifetime. The Apostle Paul says, "I'm a fool for Christ, and would rather be a fool for Christ than a fool for the devil or the world." A good question to ask ourselves is whose fool are we?

The Lord Is with You, Mighty Warrior

I'm sure you have watched the story about Rudolph the Red Nose Reindeer, and how he thought he was a misfit. While he was running away, he discovered the Island of Misfit Toys. All those toys and Rudolph himself thought that they had no purpose. They existed but had no place in this world. At the end of the story, all those misfit toys and Rudolph himself found out differently. They did have a purpose and contributed to their world. *Too many of God's children do not believe they are worth anything or that God could use them in any real way.*

> *Too many of God's children do not believe they are worth anything or that God could use them in any real way.*

There are numerous reasons for this wrong thinking, but the bottom line is that it's a big lie. It's the enemy's desire to have you focus on yourself instead of what Christ has accomplished in you by His work on the cross. Instead of saying I'm nothing but a misfit, do the work of God has given you to do. We should say what God says about us. He says that you are a mighty warrior and He has great plans that only you can do. If you're one of those who believe it would be impossible for God to use you in a mighty way, rejoice, you're in a perfect place because God's specialty is working with impossibilities.

What God Sees?

In Isaiah 55:9 it says, "As the heavens are higher than the earth, so are My ways higher than your ways and My thoughts than your thoughts" (NIV). The way we view things in life and the way God views them are different. We need to understand the way God thinks and align our thoughts with His. That's why the Apostle Paul admonished us to have the mind of Christ. He also says to examine our thoughts. We sometimes put too much blame on the devil for our troubles when the truth is, our thinking is wrong.

Again, the Bible says in Proverbs 23:7 that "as a man thinks so is he." When we got saved, our spirits were recreated, but our minds remained the same. That's why the Apostle Paul wrote in Romans 12:1–2 that we have to be transformed by the renewing of our minds. Rethink your thinking. Take on the mind of Christ as the Bible says. God is no respecter of people.

In today's world, all you hear about is that I have rights. I'm not big on that idea, but I do believe that as a child of God, you have a right to go boldly into His throne room. Not only is it a right, but a responsibility. God Himself says to come boldly into the throne room. God believes you are not a misfit; in fact, He believes that you are so important that He gave His only Son to die for you. You are very valuable.

Warrior or Wimp

One example of these different views is found in the story of Gideon. He was a young boy in a clan considered to be the weakest of all Israel. He had nothing going for him. It sounds like Gideon was perfect according to the Apostle Paul who said, "But God chose the foolish things of the world to shame the wise; God chose the weak things of the world to shame the strong. God chose the lowly things of this world and the despised things—and the things that are not—to nullify the things that are." If you think you are a misfit and have nothing to offer and that God would never use you, then you are perfect for His purposes.

Life in the Spirit Is Easy, Life in the Flesh Is Hard

A lot of times, it seems overwhelming to do what God has for us. It seems difficult connecting to His manifested presence and experiencing life-changing God encounters. But the truth of the matter is, it's easy. When we are flowing in the Spirit, we know that we are operating in a different place. We are in tune with what God is doing and times like that are awesome.

Am I Really Made for God Encounters?

You are created to display God's ability to the world. God's work is by nature supernatural, just because of His nature. Anything God does in you and through you will supersede the natural and impact the world to conform to His will. In the book of Ephesians we read, "And He gave some, apostles; and some, prophets; and some, evangelists; and some, pastors and teachers; For the perfecting of the saints, for the work of the ministry, for the edifying of the body of Christ" (Ephesians 4:11–12, KJV). He gave them for you so that you can do the work of the ministry, not just the pastors and evangelists. Somehow, we got this truth backward, and we think the professional ministers should only do the work of the ministry and be used in mighty God encounters. If you were the only person on earth who needed redemption from the work of Christ on the cross, He would have died for you. Why, then, would you say that because there are all these other people in the world that can do this work, you will not take it seriously or do the work of the ministry yourself? That seems kind of selfish and way off God's plan for you. He needs you and has work and assignments that only you can do.

God Has No Grandchildren Only Sons and Daughters—Taking Ownership of Our Father's Kingdom

As was stated before, it is the Father's good pleasure to give you the kingdom. We need to personalize it and take responsibility for the kingdom and the expansion of it. "But seek ye first the kingdom of God, and His righteousness; and all these things shall be added unto you" (Matthew 6:33, KJV). Because we are saturated in this earthly kingdom, it will take focus and effort to look past the physical and into the invisible kingdom. That's why He has equipped us and empowered us to accomplish this commission. When we get to our judgment, we want to hear, "Well done, thou good and faithful servant." We don't want to hear, "There was so much more I had for you, so much potential. Where were you?"

God Sees You as a Mighty Warrior

You are a child of the Most High God. When He looks at you, He sees you as He sees Jesus. You are totally made righteous by the blood of Christ. You are not a misfit on this rock called earth. You are an earthmover and a kingdom shaker like the apostles who turned the world upside down. Start turning some of your praying opportunities into an opportunity for a God encounter.

I remember a story of a teenage boy who was used in healing some people in a grocery store. There was nothing special about him. All he did was obey God, and great things happened. The lady in front of him was in pain, and it was obvious that she needed healing. He felt the Lord say to him, "Pray for her," so he reached out to that lady and asked if he could pray for her while she was in line. She agreed and immediately received healing. Another person observed this and asked the boy if he could pray for him also and he, too, was healed. It was not very long that one of the cashiers got on the intercom and announced that if anyone needed healing, come to cashier number 10. That young man was releasing God encounters in that store, people were getting healed and God was getting the glory. There is nothing special about us, but when God is with us, we become mighty warriors because that is what God is.

Everything Has a Purpose

> There is a time for everything, and a season for every activity under the heavens: a time to be born and a time to die, a time to plant and a time to uproot, a time to kill and a time to heal, a time to tear down and a time to build, a time to weep and a time to laugh, a time to mourn and a time to dance, a time to scatter stones and a time to gather them, a time to embrace and a time to refrain from embracing, a time to search and a time to give up, a time to keep and a time to throw away, a time to tear and a time to mend, a time to be silent and a time to speak, a time to love and a time to hate, a time for war and a time for peace.

(Ecclesiastes 3:1–8, NIV).

Now is the time we need the presence of God in our lives. Now is the time where we need His power because now is the time when we are at war. More than ever, now is the time where we need to release God's presence and bring the world a God encounter.

You're in Good Company

There were a lot of people in the Bible that you could classify as misfits, but had huge and important mandates from the Lord and accomplished much.

Adam was a misfit. He started in the midst of the Garden but was cast out of the Garden into Eden (Genesis 3:23). He was forced to accept a major change by leaving the Garden.

Noah was a misfit, both in the preparation of the ark for so many years and then the flood. Noah did not fit in with his society.

Abraham was a misfit, more than once. God uprooted him from his home, family, traditions and society. He told Abraham to move, first from Mesopotamia to Haran with Terah, then to Canaan (Genesis 12:1–5) where he was promised an inheritance of land. Later, during a famine, he moved to Egypt, then moved with Lot to Bethel. Later, he moved again to Gerar (Genesis 20:1).

Jacob was certainly a misfit. He uprooted himself to Haran to escape Esau (Genesis 27:43), stopped in Bethel where he saw the Gate of Heaven (Genesis 28:17), lived with Laban in Haran, moved back to Canaan, and later went to Egypt during the famine, being rescued by God through Joseph.

Esau was a misfit. He moved from Canaan to Mount Seir where some of them reside today (Genesis 36:5–8).

Joseph was a misfit. He was uprooted from his family and home through the treachery of his brothers and taken to Egypt in a seemingly horrible situation that turned out to the benefit of Israel.

Moses was a misfit. Several times, everything in life changed for Moses: when he escaped from Egypt at age forty, moving again back to Egypt when he was eighty to lead Israel across the Red Sea, and then spent forty years in the wilderness, leading the children of Israel.

The people of Israel were misfits. As a people, they were uprooted from slavery in Egypt, wandered forty years in the wilderness, finally planted themselves in Canaan, then were constantly under threat and rescued by the judges of Israel.

David was a misfit. After a comfortable yet eventful childhood, David was hunted around Canaan and Philistia by King Saul, eventually settling down to a new job as King of Israel. Later, he was threatened by several rebellions, having to run for his life several times.

The prophets were misfits. The uprooting of the prophets of Israel was almost continuous. Many of them never wanted to be prophets but were drafted into the position by God, without being asked.

The apostles were misfits. The apostles were uprooted from their lives to fulfill Jesus's commission to them.

The early church was a group of misfits. Many were persecuted out of Judea.

The world may say you are a misfit and are no use to anyone, saying you're not talented or you're not smart enough or strong enough or old enough. It is only natural that the world would label the church as misfits. You better prove them right and not fit in their world, because we are of a different world. Our world is a superior world that will last forever and won't fade like their world.

You are not a misfit. You have been changed by Christ's death and resurrection. The Bible says that you are a new person created by God. The point is that God chooses the foolish things of the world to confound the wise. If you really think about it, it's the world who are the misfits, who are outside the kingdom of God.

God Says What?

I believe God would say, "I don't look for great qualification as the world does. I look at the heart and at the desire and dedication of a person. I deal with the impossibilities and conquer them, and I can raise up anyone to be a mighty warrior. You are valuable. I have chosen you for a purpose that only you can do, so seek My face, grab hold of My presence, and live life to the fullest."

CHAPTER TWELVE

Escape the Matrix

So we fix our eyes not on what is seen, but on what is unseen, since what is seen is temporary, but what is unseen is eternal.
(2 Corinthians 4:18, NIV)

Paul, again, is separating the two kingdoms—the visible one and the invisible one. What he wants us to do is not fix our eyes on this world, but only on the invisible world, which is more real and more powerful. We use our senses everyday so what Paul is saying takes effort, concentration, focus, and an act of purpose to fix our eyes on what cannot be seen.

In chapter 2 of the book of Ephesians Paul writes, "You were in the kingdom of darkness. You've been ransomed. Now you're in the Kingdom of His beloved Son. There's this new entity called the church. And it's been a mystery, but it's been in the mind and the heart of God since eternity past—Jew, Gentile, one new thing, new relationship." Paul was explaining to the church about the two different worlds, the physical and the spiritual.

In *The Matrix*, computer hacker Neo is contacted by underground freedom fighters who explain that reality as he understands it is actually a complex computer simulation called "the matrix." Created by artificial intelligence, the matrix hides the truth from humanity, allowing them to live a seemingly real life in 1999 while machines grow and harvest people to use as an ongoing energy source. The leader of the freedom fighters, Morpheus, believes Neo is "The One" who will lead humanity to freedom and overthrow the machines. Together with Trinity, Neo and Morpheus fight against the machine's enslavement of humanity as Neo begins to believe and accept his role.

Non-Christians and Christians both became enamored and sucked in by what the world offers. Those who are not aware of this trap fall into the belief that what is real is the world and the physical things around us. The character of Neo in the movie was rescued from the make-believe world he was living in, which he thought and believed to be real. After he was rescued, it was a process to get him to the point to where he believed the truth. But once he believed, he had a powerful impact in restoring things to normal. We, as humans, are stuck on the planet called Earth. We also need to be rescued as Neo was in the movie. That's what Jesus came to do. He rescued us and set us free from this temporary world and the power it wants to impose on us. The Apostle Paul says, "For our citizenship is in heaven, from which also we eagerly wait for a Savior, the Lord Jesus Christ." That's the Christian's real home, not this world. The Bible teaches that we are in this world but not of this world.

Morpheus set Neo free in the movie *The Matrix*. After setting people free, Jesus calls those who are His to help in extending His kingdom by revealing to the world His spiritual kingdom and God encounters. These God encounters will flow naturally from a life lived from God's revealed presence. God encounters are what will deliver more men and women from their bondage and set them free from the world's power. The struggle that we have after being delivered is much like Neo experienced. It takes time and a process to get us to the point where we can make a major impact in the kingdom of God. The church is called to be separate from the world. *The problem is the church is more like the world than the world is like the church.*

> *The problem is the church is more like the world, than the world is like the church.*

In the book of Romans, the Apostle Paul writes what I think is one of the most important Scriptures for us.

> "Therefore, I urge you, brothers and sisters, in view of God's mercy, to offer your bodies as a living sacrifice, holy and pleasing to God—this is your true and proper worship. Do not conform to the pattern of this world, but be transformed by the renewing of your mind. Then you will be able to test and approve what God's will is—His good, pleasing and perfect will"(Romans 12:1–2, NIV).

It's sometimes easy to forget that at the time of our conversion, our spirits are born again, but our minds are not. That's why we need to be always conforming our minds to the way God thinks and not the world's way of thinking.

Prior to the Fall, Adam and Eve could see into the spiritual world. They were able to walk with God in the cool of the evenings and speak directly to Him. They were able to see the devil when he came to tempt them. This situation did not last long. When Adam and Eve sinned, their sight was changed so they could no longer see into the spiritual realm. Your human spirit is awakened and made alive by Christ through the Holy Spirit once you are born again. All the dead qualities of the unregenerate human spirit are removed and in their place are the same qualities that were in Adam before the Fall and that are now in Christ. This is what the Bible means when it says we have the mind of Christ. Now, because of what Christ did, the Apostle Paul says, "So now we fix our eyes not on what is seen, but on what is unseen, since what is seen is temporary, but what is unseen is eternal." Our ability has been restored to see in the spirit realm again.

Does Your Thinking Need a Kicking?

Are you being controlled by the world? Are you thinking the way the world tells you to think? We are to think the way God thinks. The Bible states that we are to have the mind of Christ. For instance, we know that Jesus came to the earth and moved in the power of the Holy Spirit. He performed mighty miracles and gave the world many God encounters that changed the world. When He was about to leave this world, He told the disciples that He wanted this kind of work to continue. That He was going to send the power of the Holy Spirit so they could continue in His works, and not only continue in them, but do greater works than He did. But the church has a thinking problem. Most believe that these great miracles are either not for today or that only special men and women can do these miracles. They are believing what they see or what they have been taught. This kind of thinking is totally contradictory from what the Bible teaches. *God has called everyone who acknowledges that Jesus is Lord to be a person who delivers to the world God encounters.* Compare the way you are thinking and believing to what the Word of God teaches.

> *God has called everyone who acknowledges that Jesus is Lord to be a person who delivers to the world God encounters.*

> He said to them, "Go into all the world and preach the gospel to all creation. Whoever believes and is baptized will be saved, but whoever does not believe will be condemned. And these signs will accompany those who believe: In My name they will drive out demons; they will speak in new tongues; they will pick up snakes with their hands; and when they drink deadly poison, it will not hurt them at all; they will place their hands on sick people, and they will get well." After the Lord Jesus had spoken to them, He was taken up into heaven and He sat at the right hand of God. Then the disciples went out and preached everywhere, and the Lord worked with them and confirmed His word by the signs that accompanied it"(Mark 16:15–19, NIV).

Remember, don't be moved by what you feel or see, only be moved by the word that's real.

Matrix Dreaming

I think of the story when God delivered Abraham's nephew Lot from Sodom and Gomorrah.

> "With the coming of dawn, the angels urged Lot, saying, "Hurry! Take your wife and your two daughters who are here, or you will be swept away when the city is punished." When he hesitated, the men grasped his hand and the hands of his wife and of his two daughters and led them safely out of the city, for the Lord was merciful to them. As soon as they had brought them out, one of them said, "Flee for your lives! Don't look back, and don't stop anywhere in the plain! Flee to the mountains or you will be swept away!"But Lot said to them, "No, my lord please! Your servant has found favor in your eyes, and you have shown great kindness to me in sparing my life. But I can't flee to the mountains;

this disaster will overtake me, and I'll die. Look, here is a town near enough to run to, and it is small. Let me flee to it—it is very small, isn't it? Then my life will be spared."He said to him, "Very well, I will grant this request too; I will not overthrow the town you speak of. But flee there quickly, because I cannot do anything until you reach it." (That is why the town was called Zoar.) By the time Lot reached Zoar, the sun had risen over the land. Then the Lord rained down burning sulfur on Sodom and Gomorrah—from the Lord out of the heavens. Thus He overthrew those cities and the entire plain, destroying all those living in the cities—and also the vegetation in the land. But Lot's wife looked back, and she became a pillar of salt. (Genesis 19:16–26, NIV)

I always felt that turning Lot's wife into a pillar of salt was rather harsh, although she was strictly warned not to look back. But in reality, what really happened, even though God delivered them from Sodom, she still longed for that sinful city. Her heart was there even though she was not there in person. She wanted to remain in the matrix, in the make-believe world. Many in the church are like Lot's wife. They are delivered and free, but still choose to live in the world in which they were freed from, dreaming and thinking about all the world's pleasure. If you flirt with fire, you will get burned.

Separation, a Must

Jesus made it a point to regularly separate Himself from people and the world. He knew if He did not do that, He would not be able to bring God encounters to the world. If Jesus separated Himself from all of His activities and relationships to be alone with God, how much more do we need that practice in our lives? The Word of God says to "seek first His kingdom then all other things will be added unto you." Once you are out of the matrix, don't jump back in. Separate yourself totally from it in every way. We are only visiting this planet; our true home is the kingdom of heaven, and we are made ambassadors in this world. The term ambassador means "an accredited diplomat sent by a country as its official representative to a foreign country." We are sent from the kingdom of God into this world as God's representatives. We are to live and demonstrate the will of our King.

How Deep Is the Rabbit Hole

"This is your last chance. After this, there is no turning back. You take the blue pill the story ends. You wake up in your bed and believe whatever you want to believe. You take the red pill, you stay in Wonderland, and I show you how deep the rabbit hole goes." These words spoken by the leader Morpheus in *The Matrix* to Neo are powerful. We as Christians do not take any pills, but we did ask to receive the work of Jesus who died for us. We decided not to take the blue pill and to stay in this façade world. We decided to follow Jesus, and day by day, He is showing us how deep the rabbit hole goes. In fact, the kingdom of God never ends; it's as deep as God is. The possibilities are endless, and it is only limited by our thinking and our lingering attachment to this world. It's time to pray what Paul was praying for us,

> "I keep asking that the God of our Lord Jesus Christ, the glorious Father, may give you the Spirit of wisdom and revelation, so that you may know Him better. I pray that the eyes of your heart may be enlightened in order that you may know the hope to which He has called you, the riches of His glorious inheritance in His holy people" (Ephesians 1:17–18, NIV).

God Says What?

If God were here right now, I believe God would say, "Get with Me more. Break away from everything and seek My face. Get so close to Me that you can hear the whisper of My voice. Do not be conformed to this evil world and its ways, but make a diligent effort to separate yourself. Have My mind think the way I think, speak the way I speak, and show forth My power to the world."

CHAPTER THIRTEEN

Life without Limits

For with God nothing shall be impossible
(Luke 1:37, KJV)

Life without limits is all wrapped up in the presence of God. That's why it is so important to find God's presence and remain in His presence if we are to live a life beyond our own abilities. The adventure with God is as deep as God goes. He is looking for believers to go where no man has gone before. We cannot limit God in our lives and put Him in a box like the world does. We are called believers; therefore, we must believe.

How do you want to be remembered? Reflect on that question for just a moment. Imagine that you have passed away and are able to be a heavenly spectator at your own funeral. What would your pastor be able to say about your life? More importantly, what would people from church, work and your neighborhood say about you? What would your family and friends say? What would you want them to say?

You cannot just read this Scripture, that nothing is impossible with God, and say, wow that's cool, and go on. But the thing is, even though we consider every word in the Bible to be God's word, we really don't believe this Scripture. Or we say that we believe it, but maybe we do not have the revelation on it, so that it has become real to us. We subconsciously think it's too good to be true. Jesus really did not mean nothing is impossible. What He really meant was most things are not impossible, that makes more sense. I mean, come on, that would be nuts. But Jesus meant what He said and said what He meant. What this means to you and me is that we have a life that is without limits. There is no ceiling on what God can do in us and through us if we only tap into what He said. We are only limited by our own belief and by our

> When the Bible says nothing is impossible with God, this is not a promise that God will do everything we want; it is a reminder that God can do everything He promises.

own thinking. *When the Bible says nothing is impossible with God, this is not a promise that God will do everything we want; it is a reminder that God can do everything He promises.*

Life without limits is anchored to His Word. God can do anything, but He doesn't do everything. He does what He says, but not necessarily what *I* say. *Faith is a response to God. It is believing what God says.* That's why we need a revelation of what He says; it's the life blood of faith and living life without limits. It is not just believing whatever you want. It is believing what God says. God speaks and we believe. In Genesis 18:14, it says, "Is anything too hard for the Lord? I will return to you at the appointed time next year and Sarah will have a son." (NIV)

The Septuagint is the ancient Greek translation of the Hebrew Old Testament. The Greek phrase here is almost the same as the angel's words to Mary. "Is anything too hard for the Lord?" and "Nothing is impossible with God." Mary would have known the Sarah story, and she would have known the saying, "Nothing is impossible with God." She would have connected this saying with the impossibility of Sarah becoming pregnant, and she knew God did it! It would have encouraged her to trust God to fulfill His word to her.

The saying shows up again in Jeremiah. The Babylonian army was besieging Jerusalem. God had already told Jeremiah that the city would be captured and the Israelites would be taken into captivity in Babylon. But God also promised He would eventually bring the Israelites back home. God told Jeremiah to buy his uncle's field and have the deed transferred before witnesses. It was an act of faith God would fulfill His promise and bring them home, but it looked impossible. Then, Jeremiah prayed in Jeremiah 32:17, "Ah, Sovereign Lord, You have made the heavens and the earth by Your great power and outstretched arm. Nothing is too hard for you." (NIV) Again, he trusted God's word that there were no limits in his life. Only self-placed limits like unbelief, fear and disobedience restrain us.

Gabriel's words, nothing is impossible with God, were to remind Mary that God can do whatever He says. In fact, the phrase, "nothing is impossible with God" can also be translated, "For no word from God will ever fail." That is awesome and gives us freedom and courage to pursue anything we desire.

In fact, the Apostle Paul writes is Ephesians, "Now unto Him who is able to do exceedingly, abundantly above all that we ask or think, according to the power that works in us" (Ephesians 3:20, NKJV). The movie and series *Star Trek* has nothing on the children of God. You know the opening monologue of *Star Trek*, "These are the voyages of the starship *Enterprise*. Its five-year mission: to explore strange new worlds, to seek out new life and new civilizations, to boldly go where no man has gone before." Those words are awesome and the excitement and adventure that they encapsulate leave boundless imaginations to soar. But we as the children of God, who possess dual citizenship of the kingdom of God and the earth, have also endless opportunities to explore and conquer. Spiritually, we can go where no man has gone before. Ours is not a five-year mission, but is a lifelong mission, continuing as long as we are on this planet.

You Are More Than What You Have Done

It has been said that we only use ten percent of our brains. Likewise, spiritually, I believe that we have not even scratched the surface. Even right now, the universe is still expanding and our finite minds find it hard to grasp. Whether you believe in the supernatural or you don't, I think we all can agree that God has more for us to do.

I have heard, that the greatest tragedy in life is not death, but the life that never realized its full potential. There is an unlimited ceiling in believing God and what He has said. Our challenge is reach that potential and to have the Holy Spirit take us deeper into what God has for us.

You see, God calls those things that are not as though they were. God sees the invisible. He sees our potential and what we can do. I'm sure you have seen and experienced people with great talent, but they waste it away, while others, without as much talent, go on to be great success stories. They maximize their potential. Our potential is rooted and grounded in the ability of God. That's why nothing is impossible to us if we tap into His ability. You recall the story about Bob, overcoming his fear of sailing. It was easy. He said, "I just let the boat do the work." So with God's ability working through us, it will not only be possible, it will be easy. Gideon essentially said to the angel, "I'm not a mighty warrior." The Lord said to Gideon, "Yes, you are. My presence will be with you." God enjoys taking nothing and exploding it to where it has great impact. God enjoys making something out of nothing. If you feel weak and inadequate, then you're exactly what God is looking for.

God Wants Greater Works from Us

You might be thinking, no way, I have never been used in a miracle or God encounter. Not a problem for God. I remember one time, I led a team to the Philippines on a mission trip. Our main goal was to have crusades in different villages. At the end of every crusade, we would have five or six prayer lines going for people in need of healing. I recall this older gentleman approaching my line. I was hoping he would go to a different line because he looked in bad shape and could not walk without crutches. The thought crossed my mind for a second, I wish I had someone in my line who just wanted healing of some pimples. Anyway, after brushing off the intimidation, we prayed for him, and he left the meeting that night without his crutches. Remember, it's God doing the work not us. Don't think highly of yourself and say God could never use me, or I'm not called into this kind of work. Greater works means just that, greater. You have to own that verse; it is not for other people, it is for you. Do not pick and choose the Scriptures that you want to apply to your life. *The Bible is not a Scripture buffet where you choose certain items.* Start believing God for some small encounters to begin with. We will discuss this later, but one way to activate a God encounter is by saying only five words: may I pray for you?

Water the God Encounter Seed Within You

God encounters are within us as seeds and must be watered and released from within us. You're not going to be a God encounter giant in twelve hours, but you have seed within you to be mightily used by God in bringing to the world God encounters. God sees you as a giant and a warrior.

> *The Bible is not a scripture buffet where you choose certain items.*

God specifically chooses you for great works. That's why it is so vitally important we seek His presence. We must wait for His voice and direction and that we come from encountering God ourselves. When people were getting healed from the shadow of Paul, it was the overflow of the presence of God upon his life.

Abraham Was a Sun Worshiper

God took a sun worshiper and made him the father of many nations.

> The Lord had said to Abraham, "Go from your country, your people and your father's household to the land I will show you. I will make you into a great nation, and I will bless you; I will make your name great, and you will be a blessing I will bless those who bless you, and whoever curses you I will curse; and all peoples on earth will be blessed through you." (Genesis 12:1-3, NIV)

God does not need anything from you to be used in bringing the world God encounters except desire and obedience. Ability and talent has nothing to do with His spiritual work. Abraham was put to the hardest test that any man could imagine. He was asked to sacrifice His only son, but he obeyed God and became a friend of God. Abraham could have failed and not entered into his full potential. You being a child of God, how much more potential do you have. You may not be perfect, but you're no sun worshiper.

A Blank Check

"If you remain in Me and My words remain in you, ask whatever you wish, and it will be done for you" (John 15:7, NIV). This is another great Scripture with no ceiling and offers us a life without limits. Over and over again, Jesus keeps this life without limits before our eyes. When are we really going to seek Him and take Him up on His word? He is waiting for us to get to the place where we activate His words and see the manifestations of God encounters. *All God encounters and all ministry flow out of this truth that we remain in Him.* Once again, we can do nothing without the Holy Spirit. Whatever we do without the Holy Spirit, the world can do the same. That's why in the time we live in today, it is hard to tell the difference between most churches and clubs or organizations. It's the touch of the Spirit, it's the presence of God, it's the supernatural encounters that separate the true church from everything and everybody else.

> *All God encounters and all ministry flow out of this truth that we remain in Him.*

God Says What?

If God were here now, I believe God would say that He has so much more for us to do. He would say, "Start seeking Me and start waiting on Me. Follow King David's example. Lay aside everything else and make My presence your priority. You are My son, you are My daughter, you are made in My image and host My presence. It's time for the Spirit to flow out of you and into the world. This is My desire for you. Enter into these things I have for you while it is still day."

CHAPTER FOURTEEN

Gushing Rivers or Dripping Faucets

Out of your belly shall flow rivers of living water.
John 7:38

God has created us to live with a "flow of life" that is like a river, rather than being mechanical like robots. Living in communion with the Spirit enables us to live in the reality of these eternal rivers of water that Jesus said would burst out from within us:

> "On the last day, that great day of the feast, Jesus stood and cried out, saying, "If anyone thirsts, let him come to Me and drink. He who believes in Me, as the Scripture has said, out of his heart will flow rivers of living water." But this He spoke concerning the Spirit, whom those believing in Him would receive; for the Holy Spirit was not yet given, because Jesus was not yet glorified. (John 7:37–39, NKJV).

This Scripture is so refreshing and awesome. We need to get to the point where we enter His presence out of necessity rather than duty or obligation. "The grace of the Lord Jesus Christ, and the love of God, and the communion of the Holy Spirit be with you all. Amen" (2 Corinthians 13:14, NKJV). The most powerful thing we can learn to do as believers is to simply live in communion with the Holy Spirit. In this place, we worship God, pray in the Spirit and hear Him speak back to us words of affirmation and encouragement of our identity in Christ. This is the place where the Father's love is poured into the deepest part of our hearts. It is really communion, or a common union, where we discover and more fully realize the oneness that we have with Him.

Is your life a flowing river or are you a dripping faucet, in need of a plumber? In this verse, out of your belly shall flow rivers of water. God desires us to be rivers

> **Is your life a flowing river or are you a dripping faucet, in need of a plumber?**

of living water that bring life to the world around us. In other words, He desires us to show to the world the God encounters and release the life-giving presence of the Holy Spirit. In the book of Ezekiel, it also talks about a life-giving river:

> The man brought me back to the entrance to the temple, and I saw water coming out from under the threshold of the temple toward the east (for the temple faced east). The water was coming down from under the south side of the temple, south of the altar. He then brought me out through the north gate and led me around the outside to the outer gate facing east, and the water was trickling from the south side.
>
> As the man went eastward with a measuring line in his hand, he measured off a thousand cubits and then led me through water that was ankle-deep. He measured off another thousand cubits and led me through water that was knee-deep. He measured off another thousand and led me through water that was up to the waist. He measured off another thousand, but now it was a river that I could not cross, because the water had risen and was deep enough to swim in—a river that no one could cross. He asked me, "Son of man, do you see this?" Then he led me back to the bank of the river. When I arrived there, I saw a great number of trees on each side of the river. He said to me, "This water flows toward the eastern region and goes down into the Arabah, where it enters the Dead Sea. When it empties into the sea, the salty water there becomes fresh. Swarms of living creatures will live wherever the river flows. There will be large numbers of fish, because this water flows there and makes the salt water fresh; so where the river flows everything will live. Fishermen will stand along the shore; from En Gedi to En Eglaim there will be places for spreading nets. The fish will be of many kinds—like

the fish of the Mediterranean Sea. But the swamps and marshes will not become fresh; they will be left for salt. Fruit trees of all kinds will grow on both banks of the river. Their leaves will not wither, nor will their fruit fail. Every month they will bear fruit, because the water from the sanctuary flows to them. Their fruit will serve for food and their leaves for healing." (Ezekiel 47:1–12, NIV)

In these verses, it talks about the different levels of the river—first ankle deep, then knee deep, then waist deep, and finally over the head. Plain and simple, it means that people who are Christians are at different levels as far as being submerged in the presence of God. God wants us to the point of being totally submerged and overflowing. *We go into the secret place a cucumber and come out a pickle.* The presence of God submerges us and transforms us, and we just naturally flow as a river.

> *We go into the secret place a cucumber and come out a pickle.*

Jump in, You Won't Drown

In this case, being in over our heads is a good thing. It's right where God wants us to be. But a lot of us are taking our big toe and testing the water. I recently heard an analogy of a sponge on the water. It abides or stays in the water and begins to be filled with the water. Before long, it sinks, completely saturated. When that sponge is taken out of the water, the water is still in the sponge and it leaks on everything around it. That should be us. As we wait on God, and seek His presence, we are being filled by Him. Again, this is a simple analogy, but why would we not go deeper in Him? The disciples on the day of the Pentecost were sponges who were overflowing into their community. So much so that some people thought they were drunk. If we think we have experienced all of Him and understand all of His kingdom, we are deceived. God wants us to jump into His presence and experience the deep water.

Our Life Is Not a Log Ride in the Amusement Park

Some believers are just going through life, enjoying the benefits of the Christian life, but blind to what's really happening around them. They are riding on top of the water and never getting in, which results in powerless existence while on earth. Hey, they may be having fun riding in the log and experiencing the ups and downs of the ride, but there is so much more. Paul says, "And I, brethren, could not speak unto you as unto spiritual, but as unto carnal, even as unto babes in Christ" (1 Corinthians 3:1, KJV). Paul warns us, that even though we are Christians, we may not be living our lives in a supernatural way. Another way of putting that would be living by the Spirit or in the Spirit. Paul further corrects the Corinthian church by saying that they were carnal and walked as men. You might say to Paul, "Hey, we are men and women, and what do you expect?" Paul expected, even though he knew they were human, they would live supernaturally, but they were too conformed to the world and rendered powerless.

The Secret to the Secret Place

Psalm 91:1–2 says, "He who dwells in the secret place of the Most High shall abide under the shadow of the Almighty. I will say of the Lord, 'He is my refuge and my fortress; My God, in Him I will trust.'" (NKJV) The secret place is where we go to meet the Lord. *The secret to the secret place is an encounter with the Lord.* It is to have a live, dynamic relationship where we come out overflowing with God's presence. We become like that sponge all soaked up and overflowing with His presence. Prayer is not the end goal, nor is reading the Bible. They both lead us to an encounter with God. The devil is not afraid that you pray. He is terrified if you have encounters with God and become a supernatural encounter carrier to the world. *Some people pray and pray and pray but never experience the Lord.* It's a ritual to them and they expect nothing to happen. If we are not living our lives from an overflow of God's presence in our lives, we will not have a strong impact in this world.

> The secret to the secret place is an encounter with the Lord.

> Some people pray and pray and pray but never experience the Lord.

Shadows Don't Heal

"People brought the sick into the streets and laid them on beds and mats so that at least Peter's shadow might fall on some of them as he passed by. Crowds gathered also from the towns around Jerusalem, bringing their sick and those tormented by evil spirits, and all of them were healed" (Acts 5:15–16, NIV). Amazingly, Peter and the apostles were flowing in the supernatural to the point that if people could even get close enough they would be healed. Also, Paul was involved in the same type of power. In Acts 19:12, it says, "So that even handkerchiefs and aprons that had touched him were taken to the sick, and their illnesses were cured and the evil spirits left them." (NIV) Again, shadows and cloths do not heal, it's only the presence of God that heals. But the point is that Peter and Paul were so filled and overfilled with God's presence that they were spilling over and naturally releasing God encounters. That is the weapon of His presence. Supernatural acceleration is going to come to the body of Christ. Just like the days of the early church, God's children are going to be passing by sick people and miracles and the supernatural will be activated.

God Says What?

I believe God would say, "Do not leave the secret place without an experience with Me. All I want is to have a real relationship with you, for that is why I created you. You can hear Me; it is possible to know My words. Most of My children just need to be quiet and be still and wait in My presence. Enjoy Me as I enjoy you. For in My presence is the fullness of joy. If you are not experiencing joy, then get closer to My presence."

CHAPTER FIFTEEN

Release God's Power

For the kingdom of God is not in word, but in power.
(1 Corinthians 4:20, NKJV)

"For the kingdom of God is not in word, but in power." That is a loaded Scripture we must deal with and not kick it down the road. What does it mean, "not in word but in power?" I believe Jesus answers that for us in John 14:11 when He says, "Believe Me that I am in the Father, and the Father in Me: or else believe Me for the very works' sake." (KJV) Also in John 5:36 it states, "But I have greater witness than that of John: for the works which the Father hath given Me to finish, the same works that I do, bear witness of Me, that the Father hath sent Me." (KJV) Jesus was demonstrating the kingdom in power and turned the focus of the people to the works that He was doing. It is the gospel when we release works to go along with our teaching and preaching. If supernatural works are not following us, we must examine ourselves and ask the Holy Spirit to reveal it to us and what we must do.

Think about it, what good is the power of God in heaven? Of course, it will be manifested there, and actively working, but we need His power in the here and now. God, realizing this, orchestrated everything we need to operate in His power on earth. Jesus said, "I must work the works of Him that sent Me, while it is day: the night cometh, when no man can work" (John 9:4, KJV). We only have so much time while we are on earth to activate God encounters. We must demonstrate to the world God's power. One of two things could happen, God could take us home to heaven or Jesus could return. In either case, we will be in our new bodies and in the presence of the Lord. At that point, it will be too late to demonstrate His power to the world. His power is for us today. So it is with a sense of urgency that God compels us to release His presence into the world now, while we still have the chance and opportunity to do so.

Remove the supernatural from Christianity and you no longer have Christianity. Without the miraculous and the supernatural, all that would remain are the genealogies and the begets; you would have very few pages left of the Holy Bible. Still, many Christians deny present-day experiences related to the spiritual world. At best, they are fearful of the supernatural realm, reluctant to talk about it, and warn others to stay away. At the same time, the world is intrigued with the spiritual realm. Popular television programs are incorporating supernatural phenomena and paranormal experiences into their stories. Young people are being reared on videos portraying every aspect of the invisible dimension. Occult and mystical teachings are a part of their daily diets. The world is paying money to witness mystical phenomena reported in magazines and portrayed in our movie theatres. We are spirits, we live in a body and we have souls. We have to be more alert in walking in the spirit realm as we occupy space in this physical world. The Bible clearly teaches we are not of this world so we must stop acting like the world.

Wait for My Power

The book of Luke records, "And now I will send the Holy Spirit, just as My Father promised. But stay here in the city until the Holy Spirit comes and fills you with power from heaven." (Luke 24:49, NLT) Jesus told His disciples not to do anything without His power. Today, so much is being attempted without the power of the Holy Spirit. Jesus knew that they needed the power of the Holy Spirit to accomplish anything. God had promised to equip and empower His followers while on earth to accomplish His will. It's funny that there are some folks who believe that miracles, signs and wonders are not for today, and that we will only experience those things when we get to heaven. I think we will not need healing miracles in heaven. I believe that we need them now while there are sick people on earth. People in heaven will not need to be delivered; and while in heaven, we will not be in need of healing, but we certainly need all those things while in this world.

What Happens Without Power

In the book of Acts, there is a funny story that reveals a great spiritual truth.

Now, there were some itinerant Jewish exorcists who tried to invoke the name of the Lord Jesus over those with evil spirits. They would say, "I bind you by Jesus, whom Paul proclaims." The seven sons of Sceva were the ones doing this. Eventually, one of the evil spirits answered them, "Jesus I know, and I know about Paul, but you, who are you?" (Acts 19:13-15, NLT)

What happened next was the demon jumped on all seven sons and beat them to the point that they ran out of the building naked and defeated. Jesus and Paul cast out demons many times, but they had the power of God being released in their lives. These sons observed Paul several times and thought if he could do that, they also could do it. They learned the hard way. When dealing with anything spiritual, we need spiritual power, which only comes from the Holy Spirit. It's also worth nothing that they did everything the way they saw the Apostle Paul do it. Again, there is a lot of imitation taking place in the church, but little real power.

Thy Will Be Done on Earth, as It Is in Heaven

The Bible makes it clear as day that God's will is to be done on earth as it is in heaven. We do not have to wait to get to heaven to release God's power, and in fact, God does not want us to. God is so excited about releasing His power on earth that He is searching the whole world to do so. "For the eyes of the Lord run to and fro throughout the whole earth, to shew Himself strong in the behalf of them whose heart is perfect toward Him" (2 Chronicles 16:9, KJV). In 2 Corinthians, we see a long list of the sufferings that came Paul's way during his time as a minister of the gospel. Starting in 2 Corinthians 11:24, Paul writes,

> "Five times I received at the hands of the Jews the forty lashes less one. Three times I was beaten with rods. Once I was stoned. Three times I was shipwrecked; a night and a day I was adrift at sea; on frequent journeys, in danger from rivers, danger from robbers, danger from my own people, danger from Gentiles, danger in the city, danger in the wilderness, danger at sea, danger from false brothers; in toil and hardship, through many a sleepless night, in hunger and thirst, often without food, in cold and exposure. And, apart from other things, there is the daily pressure on me of my anxiety for all the churches." (2 Corinthians 11:24-29, ESV)

Paul was so committed to the call God had placed upon him that he continued the work even as he faced such pains. The cost did not deter him. Christ was more precious to him than anything else.

This passage about Paul reminds me of the quote by D.L. Moody, "The world has yet to see what God will do with a man fully consecrated to Him." That certainly was Paul's desire to live his life for someone else, no matter the cost. As he pursued this goal being used by God, Paul helped to change the world. And that is just what will happen when one gives himself fully to God. When we stop living according to the flesh and start crucifying the flesh, then the power of God will be released in our lives. I heard someone say once that the fire does not come until the sacrifice is laid. We must be totally surrendered to God for what He wants to do and not what we want to do. Jesus clearly states pick up your cross and follow Him. Once again, when you pick up your cross and crucify the flesh, do not forget the nails.

The devil, or God's enemy, has no power whatsoever. But what he does is cause confusion and plant doubt on the will of God for our lives. This doubt and confusion renders us ineffective and brings damage upon His kingdom. Jesus came to restore all that was lost in the Fall of man. That includes fellowship with our Father and also authority which was taken back and given to the disciples and the church when Jesus ascended to heaven.

There Is No War or Enemy in Heaven

We are in a war both physically and spiritually. That's why the power has been sent to His children on earth. After two thousand years of church history, we should be at the point that if anything happens supernaturally, that it should be considered as natural. But it's sad to say that when we do have an encounter with God, that we are shocked and we consider it not normal. *We need to get to the point that our lives are naturally supernatural.* "The weapons we fight with are not the weapons of the world. On the contrary, they have divine power to demolish strongholds" (2 Corinthians 10:4, NIV). We are desperately dependent on the gifts of the Spirit. These gifts have been given to the ones who believe. They are not for us, but to be used through us for the destruction of the works of the devil and the expansion of God's kingdom. We need to sober up and realize that we are in

> *We need to get to the point that our lives are naturally supernatural.*

a great war between two kingdoms. We are caught right in the middle. That's why power has been given to us to use. If we do not use God's power, we will be like the seven sons of Sceva, defeated and ineffective, trying to accomplish spiritual work with physical strength, and that just does not work.

To Pray or Not to Pray

Jesus told us to heal the sick, not pray for the sick. When He sent out the disciples, He said heal the sick. He did not say pray for the sick. That statement might rattle a few people. That statement might get you kicked out of most churches today, but these are the exact words of our Lord Jesus Christ. And this is precisely why more people don't see the miraculous results they're praying for. Sometimes, our prayers are acts of unbelief instead of an act of faith. Have you ever been asked to pray for someone and think to yourself, yeah right, like that is going to happen! But you pray anyway just because. *In many cases we should be declaring, but instead, we decide to pray.* Jesus never prayed for anyone that He ministered to for healing or deliverance. He was always releasing the authority of the kingdom. Some in the church aren't taking their authority and commanding God's power. They are just going through the motions and asking God to do what He wants to do. But He has already revealed His will on most issues. We release the power of God in one way, through the authority that He has given us.

Authority vs. Prayer

The story of the Roman centurion's great faith is rooted in the recognition of the authority of a greater kingdom, the kingdom of God.

> When Jesus had entered Capernaum, a centurion came to him, asking for help. "Lord," he said, "my servant lies at home paralyzed and in terrible suffering." Jesus said to him, "I will go and heal him." (Notice Jesus said heal him and not pray for him) The centurion replied, "Lord, I do not deserve to have you come under my roof. But just say the word, and my servant will be healed. For I myself am a man under authority, with soldiers under me.

> I tell this one, 'Go,' and he goes; and that one, 'Come,' and he comes. I say to my servant, 'Do this,' and he does it." When Jesus heard this, He was astonished and said to those following Him, "I tell you the truth, I have not found anyone in Israel with such great faith. I say to you that many will come from the east and the west, and will take their places at the feast with Abraham, Isaac and Jacob in the kingdom of heaven. But the subjects of the kingdom will be thrown outside, into the darkness, where there will be weeping and gnashing of teeth." Then Jesus said to the centurion, "Go! It will be done just as you believed it would." And his servant was healed at that very hour. (Matthew 8:5–13, NIV)

When the centurion said, "I too am a man under authority," what he was saying was, "Jesus I recognize You have authority and this authority comes from another kingdom." Jesus was releasing the power of God by the authority of the kingdom of God. This authority works by submission to the higher authority. The more you are submitted, the more you move in authority and power. So what this centurion saw and what amazed Jesus, was that he not only knew how faith worked, but he comprehended and understood why it worked. This caused Jesus to say I have not found so much faith in all of Israel.

Elijah's God Encounter

The story of Elijah and the prophets of Baal is exactly what we need to do in this present time. God's church is consistently challenged. Many times, we come up short in displaying God's power. After a drought of three years, Elijah presented himself to Ahab, the king of Israel, with the promise that the Lord would provide rain. Elijah then challenged 450 prophets of Baal and 400 prophets of Asherah to a contest on Mount Carmel. "Elijah came to all the people, and said, 'How long will you falter between two opinions? If the Lord is God, follow Him; but if Baal, follow him.' But the people answered him not a word" (1 Kings 18:21, NIV). Each side made sacrifices to their god without building a fire. The lighting of the fire was to be performed by the strongest god and would thus reveal Jehovah as the true God. Baal was silent. Elijah mocked the prophets of Baal and said, "Cry aloud, for he is a god; either he is meditating, or he is busy, or he is on a journey, or perhaps he is sleeping and must be awakened" (1 Kings 18:27, NIV). We need to have this kind of attitude as Elijah did. King David also portrayed this kind of attitude when he said to the armies of Israel, "Who is this guy who defies the armies of God?" He was talking about Goliath. David was stunned that this standoff was even taking place. Elijah poured a large amount of water over his sacrifice and asked Jehovah to reveal Himself by consuming the sacrifice. "Then the fire of the Lord fell and consumed the burnt sacrifice, and the wood and the stones and the dust, and it licked up the water that was in the trench" (1 Kings 18:38, NIV). When the people saw the clear victory of Jehovah, they fell on their faces and said, "The Lord, He is God! The Lord, He is God!"

Elijah then commanded the people to seize the prophets of Baal and to not let one of them escape. The prophets of Baal were then seized and "Elijah brought them down to the Brook Kishon and executed them there" (1 Kings 18:40, NIV). God then sent the rain He had promised, and the drought ended (1 Kings 18:41–46). The time is now, more than ever, for encounters like this to take place. Not when we get to heaven and have no enemy!

Dynamite Power

But you will receive power when the Holy Spirit comes on you; and you will be My witnesses in Jerusalem, and in all Judea and Samaria, and to the ends of the earth. (Acts 1:8, NIV) The Greek word for power here is the word *dunamis*. *Dunamis* is used 120 times in the New Testament. Loosely, the word refers to strength, power, or ability. It is the root word of our English words dynamite, dynamo and dynamic. So what we have in us is dynamite power. This dynamite is not just to lay dormant, but to be used in our lifetime. This power, when it is released, falls into the realm of mighty miracles, healing and supernatural activities. It's beyond human power and it is a supernatural power. That's what the word means in Greek. In Ephesians, Paul uses *dunamis* in this verse, "Now to Him who is able to do exceedingly abundantly above all

> The Greater Battles, the Greater Victories and God Encounters

that we ask or think, according to the power that works in us" (Ephesians 3:20, NKJV). Also in Matthew, it says, "Now it came to pass, when Jesus had finished these parables, that He departed from there. When He had come to His own country, He taught them in their synagogue, so that they were astonished and said, 'Where did this Man get this wisdom and these mighty works?'" (Matthew 13:53-54, NKJV). The word for mighty works is the word *dunamis*. This is the power that God promised us and that He sent when Jesus left the earth. This power has been given to you and me to use and release into this world for God's glory. Dynamite power is for mountains, not mole hills.

Dangerous Neglect

> "But know this, that in the last days perilous times will come: For men will be lovers of themselves, lovers of money, boasters, proud, blasphemers, disobedient to parents, unthankful, unholy, unloving, unforgiving, slanderers, without self-control, brutal, despisers of good, traitors, headstrong, haughty, lovers of pleasure rather than lovers of God, having a form of godliness but denying its power. And from such people turn away!" (2 Timothy 3:1–5, NKJV).

Again, that word for power is *dunamis*. Paul warns about a church without power. This passage, written over two thousand years ago, nails our present-day society and church. We cannot continue on this course of a weak, impotent church. We must come to a place where we are totally dependent on this *dunamis* supernatural power. Again, we owe the world God encounters. That's our commission, our responsibility and we cannot do it without *dunamis* power. Really, the world does not need or want anything that you have to offer, but it does need and want what's inside of you, the presence of God flowing out of us as a mighty river. Satan says go to church and

Dynamite Power Is for Mountains, Not Mole Hills

Satan Says Go to Church and Pray, Just Don't Display Dunamis Power

pray, just don't display *dunamis* power.

Jesus, Our Example

It is very important to get the truth down that Jesus did everything as a man. He laid down His divinity while on earth.

> Who, being in very nature God, did not consider equality with God something to be used to His own advantage; rather, He made Himself nothing by taking the very nature of a servant being made in human likeness. Being in appearance as a man, He humbled Himself by becoming obedient to death, even death on a cross! Therefore, God exalted Him to the highest place and gave Him the name that is above every name, that at the name of Jesus every knee should bend in heaven and on earth and under the earth, and every tongue acknowledge that Jesus Christ is Lord to the glory of God the Father (Philippians 2:7–11, NIV).

If you think further on this subject, ask yourself why would Jesus need the Holy Spirit continually, if He did anything as God, while on earth. He would have no need for the Holy Spirit if He did not lay down His divinity. In Luke it says, "The Spirit of the Lord is on Me, because He has anointed Me to proclaim good news to the poor. He has sent Me to proclaim freedom for the prisoners and recovery of sight for the blind, to set the oppressed free." (Luke 4:18, NIV) Why would God—and Jesus was God—need the power of God from the Holy Spirit, while on earth? He needed the Holy Spirit because He did everything as a man, and to show us how we ought to live. Jesus gave them this answer in John 5:19: "Very truly I tell you, the Son can do nothing by Himself; He can do only what He sees His Father doing, because whatever the Father does the Son also does." (NIV) We have the same power as Jesus had available to us.

> **We Have the Same Power Available to Us, as Jesus Did**

The Five Word Activation Question

We discussed this earlier very briefly, but just saying five words to someone will activate a God encounter if directed by the Lord. They asked can I pray for you? Most people will not object to that question, but it will initiate the activity of the Holy Spirit and begin spiritual activity in the atmosphere. I would venture to guess that most everyone who is a child of God has had an inner nudge or prodding or feeling to step out in faith and engage someone that the Lord had put on our hearts. If you really think about it, I'm sure it happens a lot. Imagine if we are really engaged and are always on the lookout and expecting the Lord to direct us daily, how much more we would be used by Him. The reason we don't experience very many God encounters is because we don't initiate or activate the spiritual realm.

The Gifts of the Spirit

Witnessing or evangelizing should not be a hard task. Jesus routinely used all nine gifts of the Holy Spirit in reaching people. This should be number one priority when sharing the gospel. Otherwise it will end up being much more difficult than it should be. If the gifts of the Spirit are never manifested, I think it would be a good question to ask if the Holy Spirit even present? There are many gifts that our Father gives to His children. Everyone has a gift and it is vital to the church as a whole that we use our gifts. We all need each other. These gifts of the Spirit also referred to as power gifts are given to the body of Christ to reach the world, and penetrate the kingdom of darkness. I'm sure people flow in these gifts from time to time and not even realize that they are doing it. From experience, I know that some people flow regularly in one or two gifts rather easily. The Lord admonishes us to use our gifts and to develop them to the point where we become experts in using the gifts of the Spirit.

Praying in the Spirit

Now don't get all weird on me and freak out. When it comes to this subject, there are a lot of opinions and beliefs. But forget all that you have heard. Let's just examine the Word of God. First, we must understand that when Paul talks about speaking in tongues, he refers to it in two different settings. The first is in a church meeting and the second is in a private manner between you and God. There are rules for the first and that is if a person has the gift of speaking in tongues, he should do so in an orderly manner with a person that can interpret the message brought forth via tongues. In this case, Paul also refers to this gift as only some have this gift. Now, people will take that statement and say, see, not all can speak in tongues. If we follow that logic and thinking, then we must apply it to faith also. For the Word of God says that there is a gift of faith that not all may exercise. But we know that all have faith. So we must understand that, just like everyone has faith, but only some have the gift of faith and so it is with speaking in tongues. Paul also says, "I wish all of you would speak in tongues, because it edifies your spirit and makes you spiritually strong." So what Paul is teaching is that all can and should speak in tongues or pray in the Spirit, but not all have the gift of tongues in a church meeting. Many will object and point to many misuses of this gift, and therefore, just stay away from it all together. But don't throw out the baby with the bathwater. Yes, it has been misused and imitated. That's because it is a truth. Many times, the truth gets imitated and a lot of times misused and perverted. But that is not a reason to dismiss what God has for us. So Paul sums it up this way, "So what shall I do? I will pray with my spirit, but I will also pray with my understanding; I will sing with my spirit, but I will also sing with my understanding." (1 Corinthians 19:14, NIV) That is balance, and if it is good enough for Paul, then it is good enough for us.

Keep the Main Thing, the Main Thing

Many get upset or concerned about all of these different types of praying. The main thing in all of this is hearing from God, communicating with Him and receiving revelation so we can more powerfully be used. In this way, we will be more accurate in fulfilling the purposes of God. Whether we are praying in the Spirit or with our understanding, if we are not actually communicating with God, then both are useless. It was mentioned earlier that praying is not the end goal, but an encounter with God is. I have a Muslim friend who prays five times a day. I asked him one time what is God saying to him. He replied that he doesn't

Praying in the spirit is like the fuel to God encounters, because it brings more power and precision to our prayers

hear from God. He gets nothing out of praying. It is only a religious thing he does, and it makes him feel good. True prayer is communication and the end result is that we want to engage God and hear from Him. *Praying in the spirit is like the fuel to God encounters, because it brings more power and precision to our prayers*, like scud missiles, that contain heat-detecting hardware, which pinpoints the enemy's activities and destroys them with a spiritual nuclear blast. That's why there has been so much controversy on the issue of speaking in tongues. If I were the enemy of God, the most important thing to do would be to knock out communication between Him and His army. Disable any or all communication it possible.

Unbroken Ministry

Again, Jesus said, "Peace be with you! As the Father has sent Me, I am sending you" (John 20:21, NIV). This Scripture should put to rest every doubt that anyone would ever have concerning miracles happening in our world today. Jesus was anointed by the Father to minister in power, and Jesus continued that commission by passing it to His disciples and to us who are in the church today. It still baffles me that there are brothers and sisters in Christ who love God and are truly His children but still refuse to believe that miracles, signs and wonders are for today.

Jesus Doubles Down

Jesus not only remained the same in His work and ministry, but He reinforces it beyond Himself and His disciples. In Luke 9, He sent out the twelve disciples to go and heal the sick and do mighty miracles. He did not stop there, so in Luke 10, He commissioned seventy others to go into villages and towns to heal the sick and cast out demons. This does not sound like a plan that will change soon. It sounds like Jesus was resolute in bringing as many that would obey Him in expanding the kingdom through supernatural works and miracles. In addition, in case we still have some doubts, He told them not only will they do the works that He was doing, but greater works you will also do. This was His intention that the supernatural would grow and increase, not decrease and cease to exist.

The Church Is a Supernatural Entity

Everything about the church is supernatural. The church is not an organization. It is a spiritual body of millions of believers, the bride of Christ. It is obvious that the enemies of God, I mean the world, as well as the devil, want to stop anything that is supernatural. They know that is where the power is and are very afraid of it. That's why the enemies of God will do anything to water down the truth. They have no power to stop the truth or destroy it, but they can confuse the issues by planting lies along with the truth to make it ineffective.

> *Everything about the church is supernatural*

Only The Special and Few Can Do Miracles?

Well, you might be thinking, okay, I see what you are saying that maybe miracles are still for today. But if they are, then I think they are only reserved for a special few like the apostles. A lot of Christians fall into that kind of false thinking. The seventy that Jesus sent out that were mentioned earlier were just members of His flock at the time. In the book of Acts, we see both Phillip and Stephen are used in the miraculous. They were not special and they were not apostles, they were only deacons in the church. "Now Stephen, a man full of God's grace and power, performed great wonders and signs among the people" (Acts 6:8, NIV). Also regarding Phillip, "When the crowds heard Philip and saw the signs he performed, they all paid close attention to what he said" (Acts 8:6, NIV). Notice they paid attention to what he was saying. Remember Jesus said, "Believe that I am in the Father and the Father is in Me. Or at least believe because of the work you have seen Me do" (John 14:11, NLT). If Jesus needed miracles in His ministry, and Paul, Phillip, and Stephen needed miracles, how much more do we need them?

Paul, when he was addressing the whole church of Galatia stated this, "So again I ask, does God give you His Spirit and work miracles among you by the works of the law, or by your believing what you heard?" Here, the whole church was experiencing miracles, signs, and wonders. The point is that God was releasing His Spirit to the Galatians and not only to special people or the apostles but to everyone in the church. He was working miracles among them when they were not even around the church. So the working of miracles does not seem to be limited to the ministry of the apostles in the early church. In addition to all of this, we see that one of the gifts that the church operates in is the gift of healing and miracles. If these have passed away and miracles and healing are not for today, why would God give the church these special gifts?

We All Like to Be Validated

The word validate means to establish the soundness, accuracy, or legitimacy. We see that God validated Jesus, "Fellow Israelites, listen to this: Jesus of Nazareth was a man accredited by God to you by miracles, wonders and signs, which God did among you through him, as you yourselves know" (Acts 2:22, NIV). God already said in His Word that He will validate you also. In the book of Mark it says, "Whoever believes and is baptized will be saved, but whoever does not believe will be condemned. And these signs will accompany those who believe: In My name they will drive out demons; they will speak in new tongues; they will pick up snakes with their hands; and when they drink deadly poison, it will not hurt them at all; they will place their hands on sick people, and they will get well." Again, if Jesus needed to be validated, then how much more do you and I need to be validated to bring people to Christ and expand the kingdom of God?

CHAPTER SIXTEEN

Heavenly Minded and Earthly Good

Therefore, since you have been raised with Christ, strive for the things above, where Christ is seated at the right hand of God. Set your minds on things above, not on earthly things.(Colossians 3:1–2)

Don't Throw The Baby Out with the Bathwater

Everyone has probably heard the saying and maybe even know a couple of people who illustrate the saying, you're so heavenly minded that you're no earthly good. But the flip-side of that is you can be so earthly minded that you are blinded from God's presence and the spiritual realm in which He works. Yes, there are cuckoo people out in the world who go crazy on spiritual interpretations and distort the truth. But remember, our enemy, the devil, is no inventor; all he can do is distort the truth and twist it and mislead people. He even tried this trick on Jesus when he tempted Him in the desert.

> And Jesus being full of the Holy Ghost returned from Jordan and was led by the Spirit into the wilderness, Being forty days tempted of the devil. And in those days He did eat nothing: and when they were ended, He afterward hungered. And the devil said unto Him, If Thou be the Son of God, command this stone that it be made bread. And Jesus answered him, saying, It is written, That man shall not live by bread alone, but by every Word of God. And the devil, taking Him up into an high mountain, shewed unto Him all the kingdoms of the world in a moment of time. And the devil said unto Him, All this power will I give Thee, and the glory of them: for that is delivered unto me; and to whomsoever I will I give it. If Thou therefore wilt worship me, all shall be Thine." (Luke 4:1–4, KJV)

The devil took some truth from the word and mixed it with some lies and deceit. Yes, authority was delivered to Satan, but he would not give it to Jesus. You can be assured if there is a fake that is manufactured by the devil, then he got the idea from the truth. If the spiritual realm scares you because of some bad experiences it, is no reason to ignore it and cause the devil to smile.

Know the Mind of God

The Apostle Paul exhorts us to have the mind of Christ, to think His thoughts and view things the way He views them. Church, it is high time for a radical transformation from dwelling and being stuck in carnal thinking to seeing the invisible and experiencing the supernatural. It's time to start living heaven on earth now before it's too late. Yes, it will be easy to live heaven in heaven, but that's not what God had in mind by sending Jesus. Our assignment, our call, our mission and commission is to enforce what Jesus bought on the cross. You can experience the presence of God now and the supernatural now. Some might be thinking, well isn't that dabbling in the occult or some evil activities? Remember, I'm talking about the true supernatural stuff. If there is something occult, then there is the counterpart supernatural truth. "In the last days, God says, 'I will pour out My Spirit on all people; your sons and daughters will prophesy, your young men will see visions, your old men will dream dreams,'"(Acts 2:17, NIV). The visions and dreams are supernaturally inspired for intimacy with God and for spiritual revelation and saving men's souls. That is God's desire and plan not just for a few, but for all. This is how we know the mind of God, through His Word, visions, and dreams and through hearing God's still small voice and impressions in our spirit. There are many ways to experience the supernatural.

Naturally Supernatural

> There was a man of the Pharisees named Nicodemus, a ruler of the Jews. The same came to Jesus by night and said unto Him, "Rabbi, we know that Thou art a teacher come from God: for no man can do these miracles that Thou doest,

except God be with Him." Jesus answered and said unto him, "Verily, verily, I say unto thee, Except a man be born again, he cannot see the kingdom of God." Nicodemus saith unto Him, "How can a man be born when he is old? can he enter the second time into his mother's womb, and be born?" Jesus answered, "Verily, verily, I say unto thee, Except a man be born of water and of the Spirit, he cannot enter into the kingdom of God. That which is born of the flesh is flesh; and that which is born of the Spirit is spirit." (John 3:1–5, KJV)

If you are a Christian, then you have been born again and born of the Spirit and that makes you spiritual. So when you move in the supernatural, you are acting like you are supposed to act. It's natural because that's who God is and that's who you are. The fact is, we are so dominated by what we see and observe that we react accordingly. All throughout the Scripture, men and women have encountered God in a supernatural way. We are created to have God encounters from experiencing His presence. Moses had amazing encounters with God like the burning bush and also in Exodus 19 where God appeared in a thick cloud with the voice of a trumpet, lightning and thunder. At one time, Moses face shined with God's glory and he had to put a bag over his face. I love Elijah's God encounter in 1 Kings 19:11 where there was a strong wind that shook the mountains, also an earthquake and fire, and finally, the Lord spoke to him in a small still voice. Peter, James, and John had a God encounter when Jesus was transfigured on the mountain. In Acts 10, Peter had a trance and saw a vision. One of Paul's encounters knocked him off his donkey. In the book of Revelation, chapter 1, John was in the Spirit. John literally had a tour of heaven and God revealed many things to him. If these encounters happened to these people, why will God not continue encountering His children? The point being God loves engaging His children and in these last days, these encounters will accelerate in the lives of believers.

FINAL THOUGHTS

When Moses says, "Who am I that I should go to Pharaoh?" God answers not by telling Moses who he is, but by telling him who God is, saying, "I will be with you" (Exodus 3:12, NIV). It's when we can take our eyes off us and focus on God and His ability, that we experience the power of His presence. Paul said, "None of these things move me, persecution, death, danger, this is because you can't scare a dead man! I die daily, dead to sin, to the flesh, to this world, and alive unto God." Once again, this book began with the quote everybody wants to go to heaven, but nobody wants to die. To the extent that you put the flesh to death will be the degree that you experience God. Our greatest battle is between what we see and observe and what the Word of God declares to be true.

A Life of Choices

"As the heavens are higher than the earth, so are My ways higher than your ways and My thoughts than your thoughts" (Isaiah 55:9, NIV). The bottom line is we have a choice before us, and it is always slammed in our face. Are we going to believe what God says in His Word or are we going to succumb to the way we feel and what we see? We need to be transported in our thinking to God's level. The only way we can do that is by spending time with Him and being filled with His presence, a continuous transformation of our thinking and our nature.

It's only natural that Christians would say they believe the Bible is the Word of God. But when they are living like atheists who don't believe in God, they are living a double life. Let's take the words of Joshua and plant them in our hearts. He said, "As for me and my house we will serve the Lord." (Joshua 24:15, NKJV) The power of choice is a gift from God.

A Life of Dependence

In the Beatitudes, the first quality Jesus listed in describing the blessed life is poverty of spirit, the acknowledgement of our absolute spiritual need. Living the life our Lord has destined for us requires that we depend on His grace and the Spirit's power continuously. The last thing Jesus said to His disciples before He left was to wait for His power. If you connect the two statements Jesus made, it sums up the whole Christian life. It is realizing you have nothing to offer and are not only weak, but in a state of poverty. Being weak implies at least some strength is present, but poverty is completely empty. In the same way, without His power we can do nothing.

A Life of Manifesting

> Therefore, since we have this ministry, as we have received mercy, we do not lose heart. But we have renounced the hidden things of shame, not walking in craftiness nor handling the Word of God deceitfully, but by manifestation of the truth commending ourselves to every man's conscience in the sight of God (2 Corinthians 4:1–2, NKJV).

What good is it to have the truth dwelling in us and not show it to the world? As the truth manifests, God is manifested and encounters take place that change people's lives and bring them into the kingdom. I remember just recently that they were predicting a gas shortage. As a result, people flocked to the pumps at gas stations, and in just a short time, there was no gas anywhere. It's very frustrating going to a gas station and have them say we have no gas. Imagine going to a steak restaurant and hearing the waitress say, "Oh, I'm sorry, but we have no steak." Non-churchgoers and non-Christians have a dismal view of the church. For most of them, they have experienced a church that has not been manifesting the presence of God, and in turn, have been let down. That's why without His manifested presence released in our lives, we are doing more damage than good. May God get a hold of the church and shake it to its core so that we will start walking as we should.

A Life of Grace

Our Heavenly Father is not up there on His heavenly throne looking down on His church and condemning it. For there is no condemnation for us who are in Christ Jesus. God the Father loves us and loves the church, but He continually challenges us and convicts us to grow into a mature son and daughter. He is the author and the finisher of our faith. He could not love you more if you had thousands of God encounters every day because He loves you right now with all that He has, even with all your shortcomings. We press into His presence because we love Him, not because we can do mighty and greater works as Jesus proclaimed. The works and the God encounters that flow from our lives are the result of the intimate, blazing and viable relationship that we have with Him. We don't have to prove anything to Him that will cause Him to love us more.

A Life of Training

I truly believe ministry of this sort, of signs, wonders, and miracles, is seventy-five percent preparation and positioning and twenty-five percent manifesting. Jesus prepared Himself for thirty years then began His ministry at the age of thirty. Joseph was prepared and positioned while in prison and as a captive in Egypt. Moses was formed in the hot sands of the desert. Paul, after his conversion, was in solitude in Arabia for fourteen years. No one really likes practice; they want to perform in the games. But the real work is in the school of God. It's a private school and a one-on-one training where He develops the man or woman for His work. He is not so much interested in programs or events, but His purpose is to train men and women for what they have been called to be. Someone once said, "prayer is the work, and ministry is only the fruit." Sometimes, we get that backward and focus on the ministry and neglect the training or the real work. We don't want the sweat and the pain of practice, and therefore, don't experience being driven by the presence of God. We cheat ourselves, we cheat the world, and we cause the kingdom of God to advance more slowly.

A Life of Challenge

Why don't we start believing God for more of His manifested presence? Challenge yourself to go deeper into God and start looking for opportunities to release His presence. Start small, start by asking God for a divine appointment once a week. Ask God to start showing you paths into His presence.

Grow slowly and steady, and don't be discouraged by disappointment. At this very moment, I'm challenging myself to fast once a week. I'm going to get a couple of men from my church to join me and to believe God will move and show up in our lives. I want to see even more clearly how God is moving and listen for His voice.

FINAL THOUGHTS

Jesus, when He came to earth, brought with Him God's kingdom. His purpose was for His kingdom to rule and have dominion over the earth through His church. Those who are hungry and thirsty will be part of this kingdom being established on earth and experiencing the fullness of joy only obtained by the presence of God being manifested in our lives.

I'm with Leonard Ravenhill when he said, "I'd rather have ten people that want God than 10,000 people who want to play church." Be one of the ten, no more playing church. It's time we get serious and start experiencing God ourselves and taking that experience into the world. One person said, and I always remember it, "Live life with no regrets, no reserve, and no retreat." After the first five seconds in heaven, we all would wish that we had prayed more, sought more, hungered more and desired more for the manifested presence of God while we were on this planet. If you are reading this still, it's not too late. There is time for God to overflow in your life and for you to experience the fullness of joy.

ABOUT THE AUTHOR

Joseph Daratony is the founder of Power Encounters International Ministries. He has traveled extensively preaching at crusades and ministering in various parts of the world. He resides in Raleigh, NC, and has been married to his wife, Kathy, for 34 years. Together they have four girls, and one boy.

If you would like for Joe and Kathy to speak at your church or event, please visit Power Encounters International website and send a request. Also, you can Email Joe at: powerencountersinternational@gmail.com

CPSIA information can be obtained
at www.ICGtesting.com
Printed in the USA
FFOW03n2002230418
46319247-47873FF